Congressional Control

of

Federal Spending

D1112494

Congressional

Control

of

Federal

Spending

by ROBERT ASH WALLACE

Detroit • Wayne State University Press • 1960

ANNEXE DE LA BIBLIOTHÈQUE
Sciences de la gestion
UNIVERSITÉ
OTTAWA
UNIVERSITY
u Ottawa
Management Sciences

Library of Congress
Catalog Card Number 60–16509
Copyright © 1960
All rights reserved
Wayne State University Press
Detroit 2, Michigan

Acknowledgements for Permission to Quote

TO Harper and Brothers, Publishers of *Bureaucracy in a Democracy* (1950), Charles S. Hyneman, and *Congress on Trial* (1949), James M. Burns.

TO *National Tax Journal*, publishers of "Co-ordination of Federal Budgetary and Appropriations Procedures under the Legislative Reorganization Act of 1946" (June, 1948), Avery Leiserson.

TO *Public Administration Review*, publishers of "Needed Reforms in the Federal Budget System" (1952), Joseph P. Harris.

TO Thomas Y. Crowell Company, publishers of *Congress at the Crossroads* (1946), George Galloway.

Grateful acknowledgement is made to the Ford Foundation for financial assistance in making possible the publication of this volume.

To my mother,
Mrs. Allie B. Wallace

Preface

$\mathbf{G}$EORGE GALLOWAY has estimated that probably nine-tenths of the work of Congress is concerned with spending issues. Yet despite voluminous and numerous studies of Congress, the treatments received by this subject in recent years may be found only in isolated chapters, historical monographs or specialized case studies. The exercise by Congress of its vital power of the purse, characterized by Alexander Hamilton as a "most complete and effective weapon," would seem to warrant thorough and comprehensive consideration. Certainly I wished that there had been such a book ten years ago, when, as a research assistant to Senator Paul H. Douglas of Illinois, I felt my way through the maze of the appropriations process. Senator Douglas was determined to cut the budget in the most painless way possible, and an understanding of the process would have been most helpful. It is hoped that this book will prove useful to other congressional staff members and also to scholars and executive agency personnel who would like more light on the subject.

This book has been written on the basis of my observation and participation in the appropriations process, my review of the available literature in the field, my Ph.D. dissertation, and three case studies: an intensive review of Senator Douglas' numerous efforts to cut the budget during the period 1949–51; a review of congressional consideration of virtually all items included in all the regular appropriations bills which authorized funds for the fiscal year 1952–53; and an analysis of a budget in transition —President Truman's appropriations requests for the fiscal year 1953–54, their revision by the newly elected Eisenhower Administration, and enactment by the 1st Session of the 83d Congress.

I am deeply indebted to numerous persons for help, advice, and inspiration, including the staffs of the Department of Political Science at the University of Chicago, the Legislative Reference Service of the Library of Congress, the Office of Senator Douglas, and the U. S. Senate Committees on Banking and Currency and Appropriations. I am especially grateful to Professor Charles M. Hardin of the University of Chicago for reading the manuscript and making numerous constructive suggestions.

R.A.W.

Table of Contents

List of Tables

Preparations for Control

Chapter 1
Congress Must do its Job

The Impact of Federal Spending

The most often used and consistently important power conferred on Congress by the Constitution deals with spending money. It enables Congress to decide the size of the Army, the extent of our foreign aid, and, in fact, the volume, range, and direction of just about all federal activities it wants to determine. Congress passes on these matters every year as it enacts the various appropriation bills. Furthermore, congressional action on spending profoundly affects the economy of the entire nation. Huge expenses for military equipment, for example, may create civilian shortages of materials such as steel and copper. The amount of federal outlays in relation to the amount of taxes collected can affect price levels of consumer goods and services. Recent federal spending has ranged between 20 and 25 percent of the total national income, and this inevitably has had a tremendous impact on the economy of the country. The average citizen naturally feels what Congress does on spending issues because of its influence on price levels and the economic stability of the nation. He feels it even more directly when he "foots the bills" in the form of tax payments. Whether the country operates its fiscal policy on the basis of a balanced budget or the Keynesian counter-cyclical theory, the total amount of money spent by the federal government determines how much the taxpayer must pay into the federal Treasury.

Both the Senate and the House of Representatives devote a vast amount of time to the spending power. Dr. George Galloway, one of the leading authorities on Congress, estimates that "perhaps nine-tenths of the work of Congress is concerned, directly or indirectly, with the spending of public money." He has also declared that political scientists concern themselves with Congress because it "is a central political institution of our country which we are seeking to strengthen in a perilous world."[1] Federal expenditures, then, exert a tremendous force on all national programs, on every citizen's take-home pay, and on the national economy as a whole. Fiscal matters occupy the great majority of the efforts of Congress, a central political institution of our country which needs strengthening. The exercise of the spending power thus looms as a function of Congress requiring a vast amount of careful study and analysis.

At the heart of the spending power is the appropriations process, although we cannot ignore the over-all picture of making federal expenditures. To begin with, Congress limits itself so that it can appropriate money only after the enactment of legislation which authorizes the appropriation. Congress must pass "legislation" and "appropriations" separately, although each House will occasionally suspend its own rules (requiring a two-thirds majority vote) and tack a legislative rider on an appropriation measure.

The federal spending process begins with the background of authorizing legislation on the statute books. It then proceeds through four phases: budget preparation, budget authorization, budget execution, and budget review. Budget preparation and execution belong exclusively to the executive branch of the government, although both interlock with the congressional functions of budget authorization and review. Scholarly treatises and government reports have dealth with all four phases of the budgetary process,[2] but currently the most vexing problems appear to arise during the period of budget authorization—the time of congressional consideration and enactment of appropriations bills.

Goals for Congress

In evaluating the appropriations process, we need to decide, first of all, what goals we wish to reach. Much of the literature on the subject fails to make this clear in presenting proposed improvements. If our goals are reductions in government spending, suggestions will be different from what they would be were we to seek congressional decisions reflecting "the public interest." These subjective goals envisage specific policy results, but even many of the objective goals involve structural paradoxes because of the nature of Congress itself. For example, since it is composed of 535 individual representatives of specific constituencies, it has been felt that Congress needs more centralized direction and control. Yet centralized action can only be carried out by individual Members, resulting in a centralized direction reflecting individual constituencies rather than Congress as a whole.[3]

The aim of this book is to see how Congress may exercise its constitutional power over expenditures with knowledge and understanding of the consequences of its actions. For want of a better term, we shall define our goal as the improvement of congressional *control* of expenditures. Since Congress has the *power* of the purse, it should control the use of this power by knowledge of the results of its use.[4]

Control by Congress over the amount of funds it makes available to administrative agencies thus assumes:

(1) Congressional determination of a desirable volume, range, and direction of program activity.
(2) Congressional exercise of independent judgment concerning the financial resources, required by administrative agencies to support effectively such volume, range, and direction of program activity.
(3) Availability of congressional sources of information and analyses as a basis for exercise of independent and informed judgment.

Congress does not now have access to nearly as much analytical data about the budget as does the Executive. Although there is probably a point beyond which additional information does not help to predict consequences of action, Congress has not yet reached that point. The present disparity between its information resources and those of the Executive's means that effective control (using "effective" as it is used in economics when one employs the term "effective" demand, that is, control in fact) is held in the hands of those who possess detailed information about the various administrative needs and the adequacy of this or that amount of money for carrying out a particular program. Even the Bureau of the Budget, which can acquire more information on programs for expenditures than any other governmental body, possesses insufficient staff to assemble and analyze the data necessary to exert complete control except in terms of lump sums; rather the determination of expenditures is highly decentralized, resting with the myriad of administrative units. There are over two thousand component units of government nestled in the vast reaches of the executive branch and some two and one-half million civilian employees stream in and out of government offices (the federal establishment maintains nearly six million on its payroll if we include members of the armed forces). At work in this gargantuan, intricate maze of governmental units and employees are all kinds of centrifugal forces, divided loyalties, and crisscrossing of authority. Lines of responsibility run upwards to the President, sideways to Congress, and crabwise to economic interest groups. Dr. Ernest Griffith, former Director of the Legislative Reference Service of the Library of Congress, has labelled the result of these diverse forces "government by whirlpools,"[5] which cause dispersive legislation, dispersive administration, and, *in toto*, a dispersive state. Another student of Congress, James M. Burns, has declared that policy and administrative responsibilities are "shrouded in a fantastically complicated network of ever-shifting relationships among President, administrators, staff agencies, Senate, House of Representatives, committees, subcommittees, chairman, individual legislators, and among infinite combinations and permutations thereof."[6]

Even supposing that unit or agency heads could resolve and unify the multitude of centrifugal forces at work on policy and administration, the problem of control would not vanish. Edward C. Banfield has characterized the federal budget as

> hardly more than an accumulation of bits and pieces gathered up from the various bureaus. Each bit or piece is designed, at least in the main element of its structure, by use and wont, by the pressure of special interests, and by decisions of bureau chiefs— decisions which, while by no means capricious, are for the purpose of national budgeting often, perhaps generally, irrational....[7]

The allegation of inherent irrationality (or nonrationality) in the fiscal and budgetary decisions of bureau chiefs reflects neither on their ability nor on their integrity. An effective administrator will quite naturally feel strongly about the importance of the program he directs and, consequently, that it should have more money than it has.[8]

Any large organization must depend on a hierarchy for carrying out its functions. In this sense, we cannot hope to achieve centralized control independent of the judgments of those far down on the organizational pyramid, nor would we want an organization which failed to make use of the judgments of specialists. Still, since we must temper the specialist's opinions with oversight of his administrative efficiency, the social and political consequences of his recommendations, and the financial needs of the nation, we must recognize the necessity of maintaining at least a centralized supremacy of control.

Different Scenes, Same Plot

The development of congressional attempts to control expenditures demonstrates that the same problems have persisted since the beginning. Congress' power over expenditures grew out of similar powers secured by the English Parliament when that body first achieved the role of enacting substantive policies. Parliament successfully demanded authority over spending because of the representative nature of the legislature. A representative naturally protected the interests of those whom he represented; he was especially concerned with how much in taxes they would be required to pay. Since executive expenditures necessitated the raising of revenues, control over the amounts of revenue required control over the amounts of expenditures. As early as the middle of the fourteenth century, Parliament began to challenge the Crown when funds were not spent for expressed purposes, and the practice of appropriation developed very rapidly. But Parliament left a wide range of discretion to the Sovereign, apparently contenting itself merely with the appropriation of lump sums for specified but broad purposes.[9]

Although we modeled our own President-Congress relationships after that of the Crown-Parliament in England, we injected a great many differences. Originally, the framers of the Constitution conceived the Executive as a substantial check on the more popular legislative branch, and provided for his indirect election to set him above the people generally. However, the qualifications of voters for participating in the election of members of the electoral college, which elected the President, were precisely the same as those for electing Members of the House of Representatives—hardly comparable to a king who becomes Chief Executive as a birthright. The only significant similarity, for our purposes, was the existence of a single Executive charged with the carrying out of laws enacted by the legislature, with a degree of participation in the lawmaking process.

The American colonies naturally favored their own legislatures over the royal governors and, after they achieved sovereignty, their legislative bias led to an attempt, under the Articles of Confederation, to incorporate the executive power into the Legislature completely. The failings of this system are too well-known to pursue here. Yet even the abandonment of legislative government under the Articles of Confederation in favor of a separate Executive under the Constitution did not lead the United States to abolish legislative supremacy over expenditures. The Constitution, developed in the wake of the failure of the Articles of Confederation, contained two general injunctions regarding appropriations. It provided that "no money shall be drawn from the Treasury but in consequence of appropriations made by law," and gave Congress power "to raise and support armies, but no appropriation of money to that use shall be for a longer term than two years."

The first Congress to sit under the new Constitution faced a new and untried system of government created by a "bundle of compromises." The most important aspect of the system, for our purposes, was the separation of powers with congressional supremacy in lawmaking and executive responsibility for administration of the laws. How could Congress get the information necessary to exercise its powers, especially over expenditures, without undue reliance on data furnished by the executive branch, which may present only material it wishes Congress to see? The debates over the establishment of the Treasury Department tackled this question. The law itself directed the Secretary to digest and *prepare* (rather than report) estimates of the public revenue and the public expenditures. Members of Congress clearly emphasized the information service the Department could afford them and did not intend to create an establishment with authority similar to that of the English Treasury.[10]

Alexander Hamilton, the first Secretary of the Treasury, did not share the restrictive views many Members of Congress held toward the nature of his responsibilities. Nevertheless, he apparently conceded congressional "power over the purse" as a "most complete and effective weapon,"[11] and his success in the formulation of financial policies resulted from his abilities and adroitness in persuading Congress to his point of view rather than from the specific powers officially delegated to him by Congress.[12]

Congress also quickly encountered difficulty in deciding how much detail to put into its appropriations bills as a method of controlling expenditures. The money bills passed in 1789 and 1790 were of a general nature, but after that, Congress specified the items more carefully. This development stemmed primarily from the efforts of the Republicans who objected to the way funds were diverted from one object to another by the officials of the Federalist administration, especially Hamilton.[13] The itemization of appropriations led to the debates over the Giles Resolutions designed to limit the degree of administrative discretion over spending.[14] These resolutions met defeat, but the amount of specificity in appropriation bills has remained a perennial question. As an attempt to control executive expenditures, the detailing of appropriations failed. Indeed, excessive itemization led to a rash of deficiency requests by 1802.

Congress apparently recognized its own failure to control expenditures and sought improvements in its internal organization. The House created its Committee on Ways and Means in 1802, with jurisdiction over both revenue and spending measures. Another committee on expenditures was established in 1914 to relieve the heavy burden of the Ways and Means Committee. These efforts to organize for better control degenerated two years later, however, with the creation of six additional committees charged with examining past expenditures of the individual departments. Duplication and divided authority continued rife until after the Civil War.

In 1820, Congress enacted legislation designed to prevent the holding back of surplus funds by the executive agencies in anticipation of later appropriations cut; the transfer of appropriations from one purpose to another; and expenditures made without authority of law.[15] The degree of circumvention of these controls depended upon the strength and prestige of the President and his administrative officials.

Between 1820 and the Civil War, few changes occurred in the appropriating process despite a multitude of shortcomings. Apparently, the difficulties encountered in controlling expenditures were not considered pressing. Congress carried on its deliberations at a comparatively slow pace because only two or three major issues faced any particular Congress, and Members had few duties to perform for their constituents.[16]

However, the quickening of Congressional business during the Civil War led to mounting difficulties in the appropriations process, and in 1865 the House of Representatives created an Appropriations Committee with dominant, although not exclusive, jurisdiction over appropriations bills. The Senate followed suit two years later, but both committees were destined to find their jurisdiction chipped away as the exigencies of the war's aftermath and reconstruction turmoil subsided. By 1885, they had lost their powers over appropriations for the Armed Forces, foreign affairs, rivers and harbors, and agricultural programs. These money bills had drifted to various other committees, a chaotic arrangement which dragged on until 1920.

In 1921, Congress enacted the Budget and Accounting Act, which was based on 150 years of European and American experiment with efforts to strengthen legislative control of expenditures. This measure gave both Committees on Appropriations the exclusive function of passing on all appropriations but forbade them to recommend legislative matters. Similarly, the Act assigned to the standing legislative committees the function of reviewing substantive legislation, but forbade them, in turn, to sponsor appropriations. The inspiration for this profound and far-reaching change in the handling of money bills, according to W. F. Willoughby, was that "the basic defect of the old system made no attempt to consider the problem of financing the government as a whole."[17]

The 1921 Budget and Accounting measure also provided for a national budget system and an independent audit of government accounts. The Act directed the President to transmit a federal budget to Congress at the beginning of each regular session, and created a Bureau of the Budget to prepare it. The Bureau was empowered to assemble, correlate, revise, reduce, or increase the estimates of the several departments and establishments. In addition the Act created the General Accounting Office, a congressional agency charged with reviewing expenditures to enforce compliance with the law.

The war- and depression-caused growth in the size and complexity of the national government in the 1930's and 1940's led to an increasing amount of public and congressional interest in strengthening the power of the purse. In 1945, Congress set up the Joint Committee on the Organization of Congress, known as the La Follette-Monroney Committee, which heard the testimony of numerous witnesses who recommended changes to help Congress control federal spending. According to the final report of that committee, "Congress has not adequately equipped itself to resist the pressure of departments and agencies in behalf of larger expenditures," and "we have failed to implement Congress with adequate facilities for scrutinizing agency justifications." The Committee favored the adoption of annual federal budget totals, improved organization and staffing of the Appropriations Committees, and service audits by the Comptroller General. It urged a halt to indefinite appropriations and the practice of tying legislation to appropriation bills.[18] Congress passed the Legislative Reorganization Act of 1946 following the main lines of the Committee's proposals.

The First Hoover Commission in 1949 recommended the adoption of a "performance budget" based upon functions, activities, and projects in place of the old-style budget that classified expenditures by character, object, and organization unit. The Commission asserted that "performance budgeting gives more comprehensive and reliable information to the President, the Congress, and the general public and helps the individual Congressman to understand what the government is doing, how much it is doing, and what the costs are."[19] Congress passed the Budget and Accounting Procedures Act of 1950, incorporating the major features of this recommendation.

The background of its attempts to maintain money control demonstrates that Congress has consistently floundered in frustration. Lucius Wilmerding's study of congressional efforts to control expenditures from 1789 to 1941 showed that executive officers have repeatedly ignored appropriation laws on grounds of national necessity or public safety and that Congress has generally been forced to sanction such conduct.[20] The study traced the "self-defeating" efforts of Congress to compel compliance with the laws by itemizing appropriations in detail, and noted how appropriations have been allocated and the methods by which control has been shrugged off in practice. The study further declared that Congress had been forced to permit transfers between appropriations, authorize the unlimited use of agency income, and set up credit corporations with separate budgets; and that the Executive had mingled appropriations, brought forward and backward unspent and anticipated balances, incurred coercive deficiencies, and escaped the rigors of congressional control in other respects.

Congress has periodically sought remedies in the forms of restrictive laws, punitive actions, internal reorganizations and provisions for access to more and better information. The fact that grave problems of control still remain, after 170 years of effort, would suggest that we may never reach satisfactory solutions. Moreover, the most effective improvements made, the creation of the Appropriations Committees in 1865–67, the enactment of the Budget and Accounting Act of 1921, and the passage of the Legislative Reorganization Act of 1946, were achieved only in the wake of war-caused congressional difficulties.[21] Nevertheless, these landmarks of achievement demonstrate that progress is possible and that the search for further improvements should not, of necessity, be in vain.

The Current Congressional Role

The struggle for congressional control over federal expenditures in recent years has centered about attempts to reduce the total level of spending, coupled with executive-legislative competition over the scope of certain programs. In both respects, Members of Congress need adequate information about administrative details in order to take action with knowledge of the consequences. Detailed information and analyses are necessary for a Member to propose reductions based on factual materials. Past experience has shown that he will not simply give up his attempts to cut spending in the absence of detailed information. He seeks his only possible means of achieving reductions—either blind cuts, or arbitrary restrictions which destroy administrative flexibility. In the absence of data, Congress often adopts measures causing more interference in administrative details than might have been the case had information been available. This brings us to the question of the proper role of Congress in the appropriations process. If Congress concerns itself with details, will this not cause undue interference with executive operations?

Scholars, confronted with the magnitude of the budget facing Congress and aware of administrative difficulties caused by congressional tinkering, usually recommend that the legislators concern themselves only with the broad policy aspects of money issues and leave details up to the Executive. As Galloway has stated, "the general principle seems clear: that Congress must concentrate on the making of broad policies and oversight of their executive, but refrain from intervening in the operating details of administration."[22] Professor Joseph P. Harris concluded that "Congress concerns itself too much at present with the details of expenditures and not enough with the major issues." Professor Harris reached this conclusion after deciding that "the federal budget has become so big and complex that the committees of Congress are no longer able to cope with it effectively." As evidence, he stated that "Arbitrary or 'meat-axe' reductions, flat percentage cuts, and rule-of-thumb restrictions on certain items indicate the inability of Congress at present to do a really intelligent job of passing on the budget."[23] Professor Arthur W. MacMahon rested his criticism of congressional interference with administrative detail on his fear of such action destroying the integrity of public policy since the Members' prime concern is local rather than national:

> Can a legislative body—the institutional virtue of which lies in the decentralized choice and diffused responsiveness of its individual members—act on details otherwise than through small groups within itself which, by their special biases, may distort the application of public policy and even destroy its integrity? Public policy must be fused from the localisms inherent in popular representative bodies; it must then be carried out with as much wholeness as possible.[24]

A similar viewpoint prevails in the comments of Edward C. Banfield, who has declared that more emphasis should be given to the budget as an instrument of planning. He has asserted that "Congress sees the budget as an instrument for exerting managerial control over the Executive and . . . as a means of establishing the supremacy of private and local interest over the national interest," when actually "the primary purpose of budgeting ought to be to achieve the most desirable allocation of funds among alternative uses."[25]

Recommendations that Congress avoid budgetary details and concern itself only with major policies are traceable to the British practice. In Britain, according to Lord Campion,

> The estimates reach the House in a form to all intents and purposes final, which it cannot change because, on the one hand, constitutional practice debars it from *increasing* a single item and, on the other, the whole strength of the majority party machine is behind the Government's resistance to the *reduction* of a single item. Consequently, as there was nothing the House could do about the figures, it turned its attention entirely to the *policy* of the estimates.[26]

American critics would not go so far as to say that Congress should not change the figures, but they would have this done only in a general way, as the change would affect over-all policies.

The British system probably succeeds in England because (a) it has a parliamentary system wherein the legislature, through its majority, is responsible for the executive functions of the government; (b) Great Britain is a country of relatively homogeneous interests compared to the diverse regional and economic interests which must be harmonized in the United States; and (c) the British party system maintains a discipline over Members of Parliament which is practically nonexistent in the case of Members of Congress.

If we consider the relative competence in dealing with administrative detail, the ability of the executive branch certainly excels that of Congress. However, many scholarly criticisms fail to take into account the difficulty in drawing a line of demarcation between substantive policy and detail. Congress, as Congress, interferes with administrative particulars for only one reason: details affect policy. We can say with confidence that personnel allocation within a given agency influences the direction and emphasis given to a general program. Rates of pay become a concern, also, since these will largely determine the caliber of those assigned to a program. Congress need not make these decisions in a vacuum. It should rely heavily on the testimony of those carrying out the program.

We come to the heart of the problem. Since Congress must pass judgment on appropriations, it holds the power of the purse. If Congress is to control spending as well as merely to exert power over it, that body must concern itself with details which affect substantive policies.

Burns has stated the proposition that "Congress should not interfere with administrative details; administrators should keep out of politics. Congress, in short, should determine the ends; the bureaucracy should fashion the means." But Burns, Galloway, and many others recognize the limitations of this conceptual relationship between the executive and legislative branches in dealing with appropriations. Burns explained these limitations as follows:

> The trouble with this formula is two-fold. In the first place, it rests on a distinction between law-making and law-executing, between politics and administration, that is increasingly recognized as a false one. In Gulick's phrase, the governing process is a "seamless web of discretion and action." The great administrators usually must be great politicians as well. They must make important policy decisions with or without congressional sanction. For their part, congressmen

find it politically inexpedient to keep their hands off administrative activities.

In short, power over policy-making and policy-executing has been irretrievably joined in both President and Congress, as a result of the unity and indivisibility of the governing process and the nature of our political system. The vital question is not whether we can assign different functions to each and insulate those functions in separate compartments. We cannot. The vital question is whether we can gain unity on broad objectives among the chief policy-makers in each branch of government.[27]

Elias Huzar has declared that "the Appropriations Subcommittees have been too much absorbed in costs and details," that "Congress itself cannot do much to correct defects in administrative management and budget making, such as employment of excessive civilian personnel and inaccurate justifications" and that "their concern with detail is understandable, but it has diverted the subcommittees from the more valuable work of scrutinizing military programs and policies."[28] Nevertheless, Huzar recognized that "the fiscal agencies in the executive branch do not detect and correct all the weaknesses in the budgets. In any case estimates involve questions of judgment even when there is no doubt about their accuracy and the Appropriations Committees have their own rsponsibility in these matters." Congress, he said, should have "more assistance to help them formulate questions to which Congress should have answers before it appropriates funds."[29]

Those who urge that Congress avoid detail after the enactment of legislation seem to envisage the role of Congress in the appropriations process as primarily the controller of fiscal policy, deciding total amounts to be expended, and making general allocations among the various purposes of expenditures. No doubt this is one of its major purposes, but Congress also employs its annual appropriations studies to review legislative policies. Thus, if it considers detail in the enactment of laws, it must consider detail in the execution of laws even more carefully since factual data can now be made available.

The admonition that Congress avoid details also probably stems from havoc wrought, on occasion, by Members of Congress who have injuriously meddled in administrative detail purely for partisan or selfish reasons or for reasons based strictly on local interests which are at odds with the national interest. An individual Member of Congress, for example, may attempt to get a constituent hired by an agency, or attempt to induce the agency to buy a friend's product rather than that of someone else. There probably always will be individual Members of Congress who concern themselves only with issues affecting their own particular districts, for the most part ignoring over-all national needs. This fact would seem to lend great weight to the arguments of those who say that Congress should avoid details. To paint the blackest possible picture, there are even instances where individual Congressmen who are powerfully situated (such as being chairman of an Appropriations Subcommittee) may demand favors of specific agencies and, if these favors are denied, hurt the agency resisting such demands by influencing Congress to restrict appropriations or bring about some other harmful effects. With respect to individual Congressmen's predominant loyalty to "localisms," Griffith has noted that "Members specialize and Members bargain, in each instance largely in fields determined by their constituents' interest and interests." The hope of the "public interest" prevailing, he says, is that the "group will prove superior to the more special economic or regional interests. . . ."[30]

How can the President assume responsibility for carrying out the laws if Congress interferes? Certainly Congress should not block the execution of the laws except by use of its legislative or appropriating powers. The Constitution states that "The executive power shall be vested in a President. . . ." The President carrys out the laws enacted by Congress, but he can also veto legislation. More than that, "He shall from time to time give to the Congress information of the state of the Union, and recommend to their consideration such measures as he shall judge necessary and expedient. . . ." If Congress enacts a bill harmful to the details of administration, he can veto the bill, hold a press conference and demand appropriate action, or privately threaten or cajole Congressmen with his patronage power. Still, Congress must pass on policies, and if these policies encompass detail, with ill effects, then the President must persuade Congress to correct the situation.

Greater congressional control over expenditures would not mean any lessening of executive powers in this area so long as the influence is not exerted by means of withholding information necessary for the exercise of independent congressional judgment on spending issues. For example, the executive role in preparing the budget enables the President to exert great influence over congressional appropriations decisions since the budget is an organized presentation of factual data necessary to such decisions. The views of the agency heads also influence Congress because they operate the program and can provide information in a context of justification rather than criticism. Even the views of the economic interest groups would continue to be effective since, presumably, they speak for sizable groups of voters. A greater degree of congressional control over expenditures would not change any basic power relationships between Congress, the Executive or, for that matter, the interest groups.

Congressional interference with purely administrative details is never justified. Congress should avoid such minutiae and permit as much administrative flexibility as possible. Having access to information about administrative details is quite another matter, however, for legislators often need such information to make a judgment on policy matters. Moreover, if such information reveals substantive policies at variance with policies prevalent in Congress, then congressional intervention may become necessary.

The idea that Congress should avoid administrative detail is wishful thinking. Congress has the constitutional power to affect details, and experience has shown that it will exercise it. This being the case, the individual Members, functioning both as members of committees and as units of the whole Congress, should have access to more information and analytical data in order to ascertain better the consequences of their actions. This would result in a greater degree of congressional control over spending policies. It would not guarantee more wisdom and responsibility in Congress nor would it assure "better" decisions in the "public interest." It would only bring about congressional action on spending issues based more on valid information than on ignorance. This, in itself, seems a worthwhile goal.

Chapter 2
Pathways and Pitfalls
Congressional Appropriations
Procedures

Our goal of enabling Congress to exercise its power over expenditures with greater understanding requires an examination of the spending process. Naturally, we must emphasize congressional appropriations procedures, but we need also to weigh the preparation and presentation of the budget by the Executive since the Executive represents the most basic information available to Congress as it deliberates money issues.

Preparing the Budget

The enactment of the Budget and Accounting Act of 1921 was probably the most important fiscal reform of the present century. Before its passage, budgeting as we know it today did not exist. Heads of the various departments requested funds from Congress without knowing or caring what others were seeking. The hodgepodge of appropriations which resulted allowed no central plan for determining a proper level of expenditures and no real idea of the relationship between the total revenues expected and the amounts sought for spending. The Budget and Accounting Act created the Bureau of the Budget, giving the President the necessary tools to bring harmony to the money requests of the various agencies. In presenting a unified budget, the President gave Congress and the people a clear idea of the total fiscal outlook.[1] The new system did not hamper the constitutional powers of Congress to appropriate money; rather, it helped national legislature to do a better job. The responsibility for spending requests was centralized, and Congress could enact the individual appropriations in the light of total expected expenditures of the government.

As the level of federal spending has risen, the process of budget preparation has become more and more complex and time-consuming. The President presents the budget requests to Congress in January for the fiscal year beginning eighteen months later on July 1 of the following year. Between January and July of a given year, the Bureau of the Budget deals with three budgets. It executes one, defends another, and prepares a third. For example, after the President in January of a particular year submits the budget for the fiscal year beginning the following year on July 1, the initial six month period finds the Bureau (a) allocating budgetary apportionments to the agencies and supervising transfers of spending authority—in short, executing the current budget, (b) explaining the new budget to Congress; and (c) doing preliminary work on the budget for the following fiscal year.

The staff of the Bureau of the Budget begins work on a new federal budget immediately after the President transmits the one just completed in January of a typical year. Bureau experts then start discussions with agency representatives about programs for the new budget's fiscal year and the problems of integrating such programs with prior years. In May or June the Budget Director holds conferences with Bureau staff to get from them a general outlook for the new budget year. Policy questions are tentatively crystallized in meetings of the Budget Director and the President, which permits the formulation of tentative budget ceilings for all agencies by the end of June.[2] On the basis of the tentative ceilings, the agencies submit detailed budgets by mid-September. Examiners of the Bureau of the Budget hold hearings between September and November where the agencies justify their requests. Then comes the Budget Director's review, which lasts from November to December. As reviews are completed, the Director meets with the President to decide the knottiest policy questions although the agencies can still appeal the resulting decisions. All final decisions are made by the end of the year in order to permit the President to transmit the budget to Congress by January.

While the process of budget formulation by the executive branch has been vastly improved over the years, it contains several limitations in controlling expenditures. Perhaps the greatest of these is not in the Bureau itself but in the agency budget offices. Employees of these offices sit in the best spot to make the most informed estimates of an agency's money requirements. Yet their superiors tend to judge them not on the basis of their ability to screen requests and promote efficiency but by the way they can justify expenditures and get them approved with as few commitments as possible. Thus one student of the system, Rowland Egger, found that:

> The greatest single weakness of the entire estimates procedure in the Federal Government is the general inadequacy of the estimates preparation at the operating level....
> ... The measure of the work of a departmental budget officer, in fact, is his ability to obtain the maximum amount of money from the Budget Bureau and from Congress with the minimum of commitments concerning its use.[3]

Another limitation arises from the fact that the Bureau of the Budget has no detailed basis for its review other than the estimates prepared by departmental and agency staffs, and cannot, for example, pass directly on overstaffing in the component divisions, sections and units of an agency.[4] In answer to a question posed in 1951 as to whether another billion dollars could be saved in the budget, the then Budget Director, Frederick J. Lawton, said, "It depends primarily on how well the agencies do their job of preparing their estimates."[5]

The budget staffs in the various departments and agencies are not insignificant. For example, at one time the Department of Health, Education, and Welfare had 202 employees in this work; Treasury, 168; Interior, 135; Reclamation, 71; and Indian Affairs, 13.[6] At the same time, the number of budget examiners in the Bureau of the Budget numbered less than 200 for the entire government. The number of examiners assigned to an agency by the Bureau depends largely on its size and the complexity of its activities, but these are necessarily limited. For example, in 1950 only 31 employees devoted their time to the Department of Defense, 3 to Atomic Energy, and 2 to Maritime Affairs.[7]

Another problem, within the Bureau, is the way in which men are assigned to an agency or a group of agencies on a relatively long-run basis. While they can become experts in their specific fields, they can also become special pleaders for the agencies they handle. In his study of the Estimates Division, Egger found that the "examiners have become protagonists of their particular bureaus or groups of bureaus or agencies, and their value in the achievement of a balanced operating program has been correspondingly impaired." In fact the regulations of the Bureau state that the examiners are to be "the champions of the agency's cause"[8] in dealings with the Budget Director. They also are expected to assist their agencies in preparing as good a justification as possible for presentation before the Appropriations Committees.

Our review of the budget preparation process thus indicates inherent shortcomings in furnishing Congress with objective information necessary for it to pass judgment on spending matters. Nevertheless, the budget preparation process provides a good basic background and starting point for the appropriations process in Congress. A review of the appropriations process itself, then, is necessary to decide the relative adequacy of the budgetary information provided by the Budget Bureau and the agencies.

Reviewing the Requests

The Forms of Authority to Commit Funds

The process of spending federal funds usually begins with legislation authorizing a given program. On the basis of these laws, the agencies submit money estimates to the Bureau of the Budget, which then, through the President, sends the consolidated requests to Congress. Congress will then appropriate funds permitting the agencies to spend. The spending authority set forth in the bills usually takes the form of direct appropriations, but other methods are also employed. In all, Congress uses ten different kinds of spending authority:

1. Ordinary current appropriations, including one-year, multiple-year, and no-year appropriations.
2. Annual indefinite appropriations.
3. Permanent appropriations: definite and indefinite.
4. Contract authorizations, which confer authority to enter into contracts and incur other obligations in advance of an appropriation: current and permanent.
5. Appropriations to liquidate contract authorizations.
6. Authorizations to expend from public debt receipts.
7. Authorizations to make loans out of the Treasury.
8. Reappropriations.
9. Reauthorizations of contract authority.
10. Reauthorizations to expend from public debt receipts.

We can see that an appropriation is only one form of allowing expenditures and that congressional cuts in appropriations may or may not result in a lower level of spending. The fact that Congress faces opposing pressures—for general economy on the one hand, and adequate funds for specific programs on the other— evokes a tendency towards bookkeeping legerdemain. Thus the Appropriations Subcommittees, and also individual Members, will often achieve the appearance of economy while satisfying the program advocates. To understand this, we must consider the techniques of approving expenditures.

We can lump all ten kinds of spending authority into the three categories of spending, lending, and contracting authority. Now, let us compare the process of federal expenditures to a large water tank wherein the water supply is maintained at a sufficient level to assure its use as needed. Thus water (appropriations, contract authorization, or lending authorizations) is poured into the tank when the supply (spending, lending, or contracting authority) gets low, and the water is drained off (expenditures, loans or contract commitments) as it is needed. Each agency may be said to have a "tank" of spending, lending, or contracting authority, but the level at which it is kept varies widely. Some agencies would have to retrench immediately if Congress made drastic reductions in appropriations, while in the case of others (notably, the Department of Defense), a cut in spending authority would not be felt until later years (by which time Congress may be persuaded to make restorations in a supplemental bill or in the appropriations measure enacted a year or two later).

Permanent authorizations to spend do not come before Congress for review during the appropriations process. Money for the removal of surplus agricultural commodities falls into this category since the basic legislation permits the Secretary of Agriculture to use an annual amount equal to 30 percent of all yearly tariff receipts to carry out the program.

By enacting contracting authority, Congress postpones an appropriation so that a spending program, firmly committing the government to future expenditures, can get under way without the amounts committed showing up in the total of the amounts appropriated. The burden of making appropriations for the ultimate liquidation of such authority is left to a future session of Congress.

All of the "re-" categories, reappropriations and reauthorizations, can be used by Congress as a method of grabbing the bookkeeping credit for savings made by the executive agencies, either by economic operation or because of conditions making it impossible for the agency to commit all of the amounts authorized. Normally, appropriations are made for a specific fiscal year only. If the agency has unobligated balances left at the end of the fiscal year, Congress may reappropriate the uncommitted balance and reduce the regular appropriation by a like amount. This permits the appearance of congressional reductions, which are not actually reductions at all.

Some programs cannot be cut simply by paring requests for appropriations—positive legislation is often necessary. For example, veterans' pensions are established by law, thus committing the government to honor such claims. The only practicable way Congress could reduce these expenses would be to enact legislation lowering the amounts of the pensions payable. This same problem applies to rates of pay for government personnel, public assistance grants to States, and a host of other areas. In effect, the government has guaranteed such expenditures by statute: therefore, it would require further statutory law to undo these guarantees.

Congress can still curtail spending in a huge area by the appropriations process itself. It can drastically cut back or even completely abolish programs by refusing to appropriate funds. Moreover, Congress can withdraw spending authority and place limitations on the amounts which may be spent during a specified fiscal year.

Appropriations Process in Outline

After the President presents the budget to Congress, it is immediately referred for study to the Appropriations Committee of the House of Representatives, where, in keeping with the constitutional requirement, all appropriations measures must originate. The Appropriations Subcommittees then begin hearings at which interested parties—including cabinet members and budget officials as well as private citizens—may make statements and answer questions of members of the subcommittee concerned. House subcommittee hearings are closed to the public, although printed copies of the hearings are made available when the sessions are completed. The subcommittee then holds an executive session (a closed meeting) at which decisions are made to determine the amounts it will recommend to the full committee. Then the full committee takes up these recommendations in an executive session, and submits differences of opinion to a vote. When all decisions have been made, the committee reports the bill to the full membership of the House of Representatives, which then debates the bill. Members of Congress may offer amendments designed to increase, decrease, or restrict specific expenditures.

After the House finally passes the bill, it is sent to the Senate, which follows the same process. After the Senate passes the bill, it goes to a Conference Committee. This generally consists of the members of the subcommittees of the House and the Senate which dealt with the bill. Here, the differences between the House and Senate versions are ironed out, and identical bills are sent back to the two Houses of Congress for final approval. After both Houses pass the Conference Committee version of the bill, it goes to the President for signature, the final step before it becomes law. Theoretically, the President can veto an appropriations bill, but in practice this is rarely done. The President does not have the power to veto individual items in a bill. He must wholly accept or wholly reject it, and since appropriations are the lifeblood of administrative agencies, he rarely vetoes them.

The Bills

The breakdown of the appropriations requests for purposes of congressional consideration usually places all appropriations for each particular agency in a single bill. Aside from supplementary and deficiency bills, the fourteen regular appropriations bills in 1959 were as follows:

(1) *Department of Agriculture and Related Agencies*
Department of Agriculture (except Forest Service)
Farm Credit Administration
(2) *Department of Commerce and Related Agencies*
Department of Commerce
St. Lawrence Seaway Corporation
Small Business Administration
Tariff Commission
The Panama Canal
(3) *Department of Defense* (Except Civil Functions)
(4) *District of Columbia*
(5) *Foreign Operations*
Mutual Security
Export-Import Bank
Ryukyu Islands (Department of the Army)

Part I. *Preparations for Control*

(6) *General Government Matters*

American Battle Monuments Commission

Emergency Fund—National Defense

Executive Office of the President

Foreign Claims Settlement Commission

Subversive Activities Control Board

General Provisions

(7) *Independent Offices*

Civil Aeronautics Board

Civil Service Commission

Federal Aviation Agency

Federal Communications Commission

Federal Home Loan Bank Board

Federal Power Commission

Federal Trade Commission

General Accounting Office

General Services Administration

Housing and Home Finance Agency

Interstate Commerce Commission

National Aeronautics and Space Administration

National Capital Housing Authority

National Science Foundation

Office of Civil and Defense Mobilization

Renegotiation Board

Securities and Exchange Commission

Selective Service System

Veterans' Administration

(8) *Department of the Interior and Related Agencies*

Department of the Interior (except Bonneville Power Administration, Bureau of Reclamation, Southeastern Power Administration, and Southwestern Power Administration)

Commission of Fine Arts

Federal Coal Mine Safety Board of Review

Forest Service

Historical and Memorial Commissions

Indian Claims Commissions

National Capital Planning Commission

Smithsonian Institution

Virgin Islands Corporation

(9) *Department of Labor and Health, Education, and Welfare and Related Agencies*

Department of Labor

Department of Health, Education, and Welfare

National Labor Relations Board

National Mediation Board

Railroad Retirement Board

Federal Mediation and Conciliation Service

Interstate Commission on the Potomac River Basin

United States Soliders' Home

(10) *Legislative*

(11) *Military Construction*

(12) *Public Works*

Atomic Energy Commission

Bonneville Power Administration

Bureau of Reclamation

Civil Functions, Department of the Army

Southeastern Power Administration

Southwestern Power Administration

Tennessee Valley Authority

Water Study Commissions

(13) *Departments of State and Justice and the Judiciary and Related Agencies*
Department of State
Department of Justice
The Judiciary
Commission on Civil Rights
Commission on International Rules of Judicial Procedure

President's Special International Program
United States Information Agency
(14) *Departments of Treasury and Post Office*
Treasury Department
Post Office Department
Tax Court of the United States

Normally, there are between 300 and 400 separate appropriation "items" in all appropriations measures. Each item consists of a figure made up of a varying number of component parts which are set forth in the budget document. Appropriations items vary in amounts from a few dollars to several billion dollars. In the Defense Appropriation Bill for the fiscal year 1952–53, a single item, "aircraft and related procurement," amounted to $12,700,000,000. For that same year, there were only four appropriation items for the entire Post Office Department, one of which, "postal operations," was $1,800,000,000.

Aside from spending, lending and contracting authority, appropriations bills often contain language designed to limit and direct expenditures. Such language often begins: "No part of the appropriations contained in this Act shall be expended for . . . ." This language is employed for a variety of purposes, such as not permitting any single recipient of a subsidy to receive more than a specified amount, or preventing an agency from employing more than a specified number of personnel officers.

Items included in appropriation bills may not be expended for other than the specified purposes, but these purposes are normally so general as to allow a considerable degree of discretion in the hands of the operating agencies. The way the agencies plan to spend an amount appropriated in an item may be set forth in a general way in the budget document, but this is merely a declaration of the agencies' intent and does not have the force of law. Similarly, item breakdowns in committee reports are a declaration of the committee's intent, without any force of law. However, agencies will tend to follow the item breakdowns in both the budget and committee reports in order not to incur any enmity of Members of Congress, who base their judgment on these breakdowns.

Committees and Subcommittees

Appropriations Committees differ from other congressional committees in several important respects. Members of the House Appropriations Committee do not serve on other committees except in extremely rare instances; membership is large enough to permit exclusive subcommittee assignments. One of the results of this system is a high degree of specialization in the various appropriations areas, with both the advantages and disadvantages that "specialization" implies. Another result is continuity, with most of a member's work consisting of an annual review of the same area, and, basically, the same issues. While the competence, fairness, and experience inherent in any given five or seven man subcommittee continues year after year, so does all the bias, obtuseness, and laziness which may exist in the same group.

The Senate Appropriations Committee is too small to permit exclusive subcommittee assignments. The average Senate Committee member hence cannot spend as much time on details as does his counterpart in the House. Certain of the Senate subcommittees have ex-officio members from the appropriate standing committees serving as liaison.

Normally the House will make severe reductions in appropriations, placing the Senate Committee in the role of an appellant tribunal or board of review. During the Senate hearings on the Civil Functions Appropriations bill in 1952, for example, Army Engineer witnesses pointed their remarks to restoration of the cuts made by the House. The tone of the Senate Committee proceedings appeared more sympathetic to the Corps budget presentation than that of the House Committee. Representative Hubert Scudder of California, while discussing the House action on civil functions projects around the world with the Senate Committee Chairman, Senator Kenneth McKellar, observed:

> From what I have been able to learn during the two sessions I have been in Congress, that seems to be the procedure, to cut over there (in the House Committee) and put it back over here. I do not agree with the policy but that seems to be the way it works.[9]

And Senator Paul H. Douglas, of Illinois, writes of the appropriations appeal nature of the Senate as follows:

> One of the common jokes around Washington is that an agency will request more than it actually needs, depending on the House

to cut its request by 50 percent, the Senate to restore the amount to 100 percent, and the conference committee to compromise at 75 percent, which is the figure actually wanted by the Agency in the first place. This is more indicative than accurate. But it is true that the Senate, traditionally, is the more lenient body. Some wags suggest that this is why it is called "the upper House."[10]

That the House should make drastic reductions and the Senate provide the increases may seem paradoxical. Congressmen must run for re-election every two years, while Senators run only every six years. It is generally more pleasing to one's constituency to vote large amounts for pet projects and programs. Nevertheless, good reasons exist to account for the Senate's spending tendencies. First, while Congressmen run for re-election more often than Senators, Senators represent whole States rather than Congressional districts; they have broader constituencies and must please a greater variety of interests. Second, the agencies and pressure groups concerned do not have time to mobilize their efforts to stop cuts in the House. Since the House acts first, the pressure groups very nearly face a cut before they can begin to operate. Therefore, they have historically treated the Senate as an "appeal" body, and they utilize their principal strength to exert pressure there. A third reason, as we shall see, lies with the subcommittee's makeup in the House as compared with that in the Senate.

The locus of the congressional power over the purse lies within the Appropriations Subcommittees, which take first crack at the budget estimates. Both the full committee and the full membership may alter the recommendations of the subcommittees, but these tight-knit little groups wield a tremendous influence since they shoulder the responsibility for item-by-item scrutiny of the bills. The subcommittees hold hearings, study the items with the staff, and "mark-up" the bills for submission to the full committee. The fact that the subcommittee members labor for weeks and possibly months on an appropriations measure virtually precludes opposition to their recommendations except on broad policy matters. Moreover, barring partisan splits or uncompromisable differences of opinion, subcommittee members will reach agreements on all items and act as a unit before the full committee. On the same basis, the full committee will act as a unit before the full membership of the House or Senate.

Since the Appropriations Subcommittees are the primary locus of power in the congressional spending process, we ought to look at the membership of some of the typical ones, to see what influences operate. Let us, therefore, see how subcommittee vacancies are filled, and then examine some actions of the three subcommittees in the Senate and the House of Representatives which pass on funds most directly felt in the States where they are expended, Department of Interior, Civil Functions of the Army, and Department of Agriculture.

In the Senate, seniority settles the question of who fills subcommittee vacancies; members with the longest service on the committee get first choice. In the House, however, the committee chairman allocates the subcommittee membership of the majority party and the ranking minority member determines the minority party membership. As we shall see, this difference of the assignments to subcommittees accounts for a marked difference in the makeup of House subcommittees compared with that in the Senate. Those who serve on the House subcommittees represent regions that have little stake in the appropriations under their subcommittee's jurisdiction and thus subcommittee members do not quaver at the thought of substantial reductions. The opposite is true of the Senate subcommittees. Since these are filled according to individual choice backed up by sufficient seniority, members of the Senate Appropriations Committee will seek to serve on subcommittees which consider funds politically important to them. Consequently, there is a tendency for them to seek increases and certainly to oppose cuts in programs dear to the hearts of their constituents. Moreover, seeking reductions, even in programs not affecting their districts, would mitigate against their chances of securing the appropriations they want for the programs they wish to promote.

Let us first consider the 82d Congress subcommittees, which in 1952 handled the Civil Functions of the Army appropriations bill, a measure furnishing funds for rivers, harbors and flood control programs. What "stake" did the Members of these subcommittees and the States they represented have in the Civil Functions bill for which they made recommendations?

As shown in Table 1, Senate members of the Civil Functions Subcommittee represented eleven States with a stake in the subcommittee appropriation bill. These States accounted for nearly one-half of the total budget requests for rivers, harbors, and flood

Table 1

REGIONAL "STAKES" IN CIVIL FUNCTIONS APPROPRIATIONS: APPROPRIATIONS SUBCOMMITTEE MAKEUP AND AMOUNTS REQUESTED FOR EXPENDITURE IN STATES REPRESENTED (1952)

SENATE		HOUSE	
Member and State Represented on Subcommittee	*Amount Requested in Budget to be Spent in Such State*	*Member and State Represented on Subcommittee*	*Amount Requested in Budget to be Spent in Such State*
McKellar, Tenn., (D)	$24,331,000	Kerr, N. C., (D)	$0
Hayden, Ariz., (D)	800,000	Cannon, Mo., (D)	12,570,000
Russell, Ga., (D)	4,100,000	Rabaut, Mich.,	0
Ellender, La., (D)	1,134,000	(D)	
McClelland, Ark., (D)	12,834,000	Davis, Wisc., (R)	0
Robertson, Va., (D)	100,000	Ford, Mich., (R)	0
Knowland, Calif., (R)	61,544,000		
Young, N. Dak., (R)	38,850,000		
Cordon, Oreg., (R)	131,850,000		
Thye, Minn., (R)	3,742,000		
Ecton, Mont., (R)	1,225,000		
Totals	$280,510,000		$12,570,000

Total budget requests for Expenditure in States (rivers, harbors and flood control)—$595,651,000.

Source: S. Rep. No. 1754, 82d Congress, 2d Sess. (1952).

control items. In the case of the House subcommittee, only one member came from a State with a stake in the bill, and that member was the chairman of the full Appropriations Committee, who named the majority party members to fill vacancies on the subcommittee. (Minority member vacancies were filled by Rep. John Taber of New York, a State which has very little to gain from Civil Function funds.) Rep. Clarence Cannon, of Missouri, the chairman of the full House committee, represented the Ninth District of Missouri. The Missouri River flows through the middle of this district, and it is bounded on the east by the Mississippi River. Of the $12,570,000 slated for expenditure in Missouri, $5,000,000 was for projects directly affecting this district.

PART I. *Preparations for Control*

Table 2

REGIONAL "STAKES" IN INTERIOR APPROPRIATIONS:
APPROPRIATIONS SUBCOMMITTEE MAKEUP AND
AMOUNTS REQUESTED FOR EXPENDITURE IN
STATES REPRESENTED (1952)

SENATE		HOUSE	
Member and State Represented on Subcommittee	*Amount Requested in Budget to be Spent in Such State*	*Member and State Represented on Subcommittee*	*Amount Requested in Budget to be Spent in Such State*
Hayden, Ariz., (D)	$9,343,000	Kirwan, Ohio, (D)	$0
O'Mahoney, Wyo., (D)	5,613,000	Norrell, Ark., (D)	0
McCarran, Nev., (D)	3,763,000	Jackson, Wash.,	20,106,000
Chavez, N. Mex., (D)	2,254,000	(D)	
Ellender, La., (D)	0	Furcolo, Mass., (D)	0
Kilgore, W. Va., (D)	0	Jensen, Iowa, (R)	0
Cordon, Oreg., (R)	368,000	Fenton, Pa., (R)	0
Young, N. D., (R)	59,000		
Knowland, Calif., (R)	49,080,000		
Ecton, Mont., (R)	19,080,000		
McCarthy, Wisc., (R)	0		
Totals	$89,560,000		$20,106,000

Total budget requests for Expenditure in States (Bureau of Reclamation, Construction)—$196,770,000.

Source: S. Rep. No. 1803, 82d Cong., 2d Sess. (1952).

Next, let us consider the Department of Interior subcommittees for the same period. The differences between the House and Senate subcommittees are again shown in Table 2. Senate subcommittee members came from States slated to receive over four times as much construction money as those represented on the House subcommittee, and, as a matter of fact, the expenditures planned for the State of Washington were outside the district of Rep. Henry Jackson, the House subcommittee member from that State.

The situation that existed in the membership of the House and the Senate Appropriations Subcommittees on Agriculture shows a vastly different picture. The membership of the two Agriculture subcommittees during the 82d Congress were:

Senate				
Russell, Ga.	(D)	Cordon, Oreg.	(R)
Hayden, Ariz.	(D)	McCarthy, Wis.	(R)
O'Mahoney, Wyo.	(D)	*House*	
McCarren, Nev.	(D)	Whitten, Miss.	(D)
Chavez, N. Mex.	(D)	Stigler, Okla.	(D)
Maybank, S. C.	(D)	Bates, Ky.	(D)
Young, N. D.	(R)	Anderson, Minn.	(R)
Ferguson, Mich.	(R)	Horan, Wash.	(R)

Thus, the entire membership of both Senate and House Agriculture Appropriations Subcommittees (with the single exception of Ferguson of Michigan) represented predominantly rural areas with a stake in agricultural expenditures. As a result, there was very little difference between the amounts passed by the House and the amount recommended by the Senate Appropriations Committee. As shown in Table 3, the Senate committee recommended increases, over the amounts passed by the House, of 35 percent for Civil Functions, 15 percent for Interior, but less than 1 percent for Agriculture.

Interior, Civil Functions, and Agriculture, along with Defense, are the subcommittees having jurisdiction over spending with a fairly direct impact on specific areas. Appropriations considered by other subcommittees are of a more general nature, and membership on them is not as popular as those we have discussed.

Table 3

COMPARISON OF APPROPRIATIONS REQUESTED IN BUDGET
PASSED BY HOUSE, AND RECOMMENDED BY THE SENATE
APPROPRIATIONS COMMITTEE, FOR FISCAL YEAR 1953,
FOR CIVIL FUNCTIONS, INTERIOR, AND AGRICULTURE

Appropriation Bill, Funds for 1953	*Total Requested in Budget*	*Amount Passed by House*	*Amount Recommended by Senate Appropriations Committee*
Civil Functions	$712,628,000	$492,435,000	$666,775,000
Interior	632,152,000	486,248,000	560,000,000
Agriculture	931,803,000	724,586,000	731,608,000

Source: S. Rep. Nos. 1754, 1803, 1619, 82d Cong., 2d Sess. (1952).

What does the above analysis of the makeup of these sub-committees demonstrate? Should not members have an abiding interest in the funds they are studying, or does such an interest make for undue bias? The answer is neither. Subcommittee (and full committee) members may be biased against certain expenditures which do not affect their districts because they feel pressures to achieve economy. On the other hand, members with a stake in such expenditures will tend to force them up. Thus, Congress should treat their recommendations for what they are: recommendations to be considered and not to be passed blindly simply because they come from a congressional committee. While this may seem axiomatic to many, it is not axiomatic in Congress. Indeed, the "competence" of the "committee" cited in congressional debates is an extremely effective method of defending committee recommendations.

The Hearings

Subcommittees of each House hold hearings on all regular appropriations bills. These hearings develop information about particular expenditures and programs, but the witnesses almost invariably represent agencies defending the budget requests or individuals and pressure groups demanding larger expenditures. For example, House subcommittee hearings on the Civil Functions of the Army Appropriations bill (rivers, harbors, and flood control) in 1952 consisted of two volumes. Part 1 contained about 500 pages of testimony of Army representatives exclusively. Another 910-page volume was required to contain all the testimony of 110 Members of Congress from 35 States and 300 other organizations or individuals who wanted appropriations for rivers and harbors and flood control projects in their areas.[11]

The Senate subcommittee hearings on the same bill required some 1,500 pages. The bulk of the hearings followed the passage of the bill by the House and consisted principally of pleas by the Assistant Chief of Engineers for restoration of the House cuts. In addition, 75 Members of Congress and 220 other witnesses came before the committee favoring appropriations for particular river, harbor, or flood control projects.[12]

Where economic or political conflicts come into play, private individuals and groups will sometimes testify for reductions in specific expenditures. For instance, representatives of the railroad industry have testified in opposition to expenditures for navigation projects which would create competition for the railroads. Such instances are rare, however, and cannot be relied upon as a continuing source of valid information.

During the subcommittee hearings, agency representatives and the staff of the Bureau of the Budget explain the various requests, but these explanations always come in a context of justification. So far as the agencies and the Bureau of the Budget are concerned, the executive branch has already made all the final decisions, and they strongly oppose any changes by Congress. Griffith has summarized the limited value of the agencies and the Bureau for subcommittee hearings:

> the approach employed by the executive retains the fiction of the equal importance of all items in the estimates, and what would be enormously valuable assistance from the Bureau of the Budget or the agency itself, in assessing priorities, is not forthcoming.[18]

Thus, while hearings help Congress and the subcommittees in gathering information, suggestions for cuts usually face a barrage of arguments gathered by men who have been in constant touch with the budget process and who have access to those particular facts which will back them up.

Subcommittee and Committee Markup

After the completion of a subcommittee's hearings, its staff will prepare "side slips," which compile the most significant data about each item in the bill, such as prior year appropriations and expenditures, program purposes, significant portions of statements, explanations, recommendations, and criticisms. Each member of the subcommittee receives side slips usually several days before marking up the bill.

During markup, the subcommittee will hold an executive session, each member having side slips and other data available for ready reference. Staff members will answer questions and take notes for purposes of drafting the subcommittee's report. The group goes through the bill, chronologically taking up each item and deciding the amounts to recommend. Often the subcommittee will pass over an item until it can obtain additional data or until an absent subcommittee member who has expressed a particular interest in some item can attend.

After the subcommittee completes its markup, it will provide a "committee print" of the bill embodying its recommendations for use by the full committee. It will also prepare a report for submission in the same manner. The full committee then, with the aid of side slips and staff, will go over the items in executive session, submitting differences to a vote where necessary. In these sessions, the subcommittee members, especially the chairman and the ranking minority member, wield great influence.

The weight given by the full committee to subcommittee recommendations is due to the facts that (a) the subcommittee has devoted more time and study to their bill than have other members of the full committee and hence are more familiar with details, (b) members of other subcommittees avoid criticism as much as possible since they dislike having others criticize their recommendations on the bills they have charge of, and (c) both majority and minority members of the full committee rely heavily on what their counterparts on the subcommittee determine, because they themselves are pressed for time and they will have developed a trust in the judgments of certain members of the subcommittees.

Each subcommittee member has his own special viewpoints and particular political problems. Thus, when they come together for deliberation, they develop a sense of dealing with their confreres, learning their biases and needs. Much has been said of "logrolling," but this practice is rarely overt. The Southerner will want river projects; the Westerner, irrigation; and one from the Northwest will want public power. The member whose constituency contains a significant degree of farming interests will jealously guard appropriations for the Department of Agriculture. Other members will want new or improved army camps, naval or air bases for their district, while still others will represent areas containing railroad, shipping, mineral, manufacturing and labor interests. Those whose political preferences need little in the way of appropriations will not actively seek enemies in Congress, since they will want all possible votes on other matters (although such Members of Congress are not numerous in the Appropriations Committee since they will concern themselves more with the work of the standing legislative committees). Intra-committee logrolling is informal, covert, and largely negative in the sense that the inhibitory factor in proposing reductions rests with the fear of reciprocal action.

The Appropriations Committees are probably the most powerful in Congress since money is the life blood of both agencies and programs. Because of the influence of these committees, they are among the most popular among members of Congress, and the prize of membership, therefore, goes only to the most powerful men with long terms of service. Politically potent in their own right, these men find that membership on an Appropriations Committee enhances their power even further—especially if they head Appropriations Subcommittees.

Floor Debate

When an appropriations bill comes before the full membership of the House and Senate for debate, the Appropriations Committee exerts tremendous power. If a Member of Congress who does not sit on the committee challenges its recommendations, he often finds himself charged with something akin to rank insubordination. Even on broad policy matters, including partisan issues, the person leading a challenge is better off as a member of the subcommittee concerned—at least a member of the full committee. Sometimes, of course, a party leader not a member of the committee may make the challenge, but this seldom occurs. Also, the chairman or ranking minority member of a standing committee having jurisdiction over the subject matter of the appropriations item may lead opposition to the committee. This, too, is rare.

A large number of Members in both Houses of Congress, knowing little of the details of an issue, will side with the committee on all questions. For example, during consideration of the Defense Appropriation in 1952, Representative Vinson of Georgia took the floor to urge early House acceptance of the committee version of the bill:

> They [the Committee] deserve the support of every Member of this House because they are in a far better position to know the needs and necessities of national defense than you and I, who have not given it the complete and detailed study it should have.[14]

This was advice from the chairman of the House Armed Services Committee.

Floor managers of money bills are not loathe to press their advantage. They are quick to point out that the committee has given careful scrutiny to all items, reducing or increasing them as much as they considered proper in the light of a great fund of knowledge. It is not uncommon for a chairman to imply that one seeking reductions below amounts recommended by the committee is attacking the ability of the committee members themselves and that it is ridiculous for an individual Member of Congress to seek such reductions because he cannot possibly be as capable as the whole Appropriations Committee.

Members of Congress will hesitate to vote with a nonmember of the committee who challenges the committee recommendations for fear of incurring the wrath of committee members who, perhaps, have wrangled for weeks reaching agreements among themselves. These committee members have little patience with nonmembers who vote to upset tenuous committee compromises on amounts and question the judgment of the committee. The challenger and those supporting him are likely to find unsympathetic ears if they ever appear before the committee seeking new or increased funds for some particular object. This is especially true of those seeking reductions. Those seeking increases are viewed more tolerantly since there is a mutual understanding of the need to please constituents and the fact that interest groups will "remember" if a Member of Congress opposes increases for their favorite agencies and programs. On the other hand, advocates of economy in general find it difficult to become aroused over individual items involving relatively small amounts of money.

Thus a great gulf separates Members of Congress who sit on Appropriations Committees and those who do not. During the committee consideration of an appropriation bill, compromises and agreements are worked out. When the bill comes before Congress, Members who are not on the Appropriations Committees find themselves faced with still another pressure group. For the committees generally present themselves as a solid front to oppose any changes in the bill. In this respect, the committee recommendations become like those of the Bureau of the Budget: "All items have been carefully scrutinized, and all possible reductions have been made."

The subcommittee chairmen act as floor managers for the bills which they have reviewed. They initiate the debate with a statement justifying the committee's actions. Then the House or Senate proceeds to the consideration of committee amendments, which are changes in the bill recommended by the Appropriations Committee. Committee amendments are themselves open to amendment from the floor.

Normally, all committee amendments will be passed, amended, or rejected before floor amendments are considered. When all amendments have been acted on, the bill receives a third reading and is passed. Although a few Members will vote against an appropriation bill if it is subjected to a roll call vote, such a bill virtually never fails to pass since a vote against the bill means a vote against every program for which it carries funds. If there are deep issues which cannot be resolved by amendment, a motion will be made to recommit the bill to the committee, usually with instructions to report it back with some type of change.

As in the case of the committees, logrolling among the entire membership of a House of Congress is both covert and negative. One Member of Congress, a Southerner, once frankly stated privately that he could not vote for any reduction on reclamation projects since the Westerners might retaliate by voting for cuts in rivers, harbors, and flood control funds. This remark characterizes the attitude of many Members of Congress generally, but especially members of the Appropriations Committees. No Member wants to make enemies unless absolutely necessary. The most consistently active economy advocates in the Senate during the 81st and 82d Congresses were Senators Styles Bridges of New Hampshire, Homer Ferguson of Michigan, and Paul H. Douglas of Illinois. The first two were conservative Republicans, representing States receiving little in the way of appropriations, without an especial interest in agriculture, welfare, foreign aid, or strong defense programs. Although Senator Douglas was an advocate of the aforementioned programs, and although his State of Illinois had a stake in federal funds for rivers and harbors, it is nevertheless true that Illinois is a relatively rich state and receives proportionately very little in funds when compared to the vast majority of the other States. The same picture may be found on the issue of economy, generally. States of the North and Northeast, such as Illinois, Michigan, Indiana, Ohio, Pennsylvania, New Jersey, Delaware, New York, Connecticut, New Hampshire, Maine, and Vermont, gain little from federal appropriations, and it is Members of Congress from these areas that seem to account for the bulk of "economy" votes.

Conference Committee

After an appropriations bill has been passed by both Houses of Congress, a conference committee meets to iron out the differences between the two versions. Here, again, the subcommittees wield great power, for Appropriations Conference Committees are composed of members of the appropriate appropriations subcommittees. Thus, even if the committee recommendations have been altered by floor action, the subcommittee members may strive for a return to their original determinations in the conference. When the report of the Conference Committee is presented for approval, it cannot be amended on the floor of either House—it must be completely accepted or rejected (although it may be rejected and sent back to conference with specific instructions). Because of the urgency of appropriations bills, there is an abundant amount of pressure for quick approval.

SUMMARY

Although far from perfect, the appropriations process itself presents few really troublesome problems. Nevertheless, reviewing the process points up glaring difficulties which face Members of Congress, especially those who do not serve on Appropriations Committees. The problem of control, in having access to sufficient information to take action with knowledge of the consequences, looms large.

The congressional difficulties in assessing money issues begin during the formulation of the federal budget, prepared exclusively by the executive branch of the government, which tends to work in behalf of the agency interests. After the President presents the budget to Congress, the agencies and the Bureau of the Budget maintain the fiction that all estimates are equally sound. It becomes the "President's budget" so that agency and Bureau representatives will explain it only in a context of justification. Criticism by these officials of any of the features would be construed as an attack on the President's program. Thus Congress cannot rely on agency and Bureau personnel for objective commentary on the executive requests.

Witnesses at hearings normally represent agencies or private groups interested only in justifying the budget requests or seeking even higher appropriations. And there is, of necessity, too much reliance on members of the Appropriations Committees involving the twofold problem of representation of narrow interests and lack of information itself.

Chapter **3**

Making up its Mind
Congressional Facilities for
Control

Since we entrust the spending power with Congress, let us review the facilities available as aids to Congress in exercising its independent judgment on expenditures. We would not ask a secretary to type a letter on a faulty typewriter, a mechanic to make automobile repairs without wrenches, or any person or group to perform any type of task without adequate tools. An assigned function obviously can best be carried out if facilities are provided to enable the assignee to do his job expeditiously with all possible knowledge of its implications.

The importance of congressional facilities for passing on spending issues thus leads us to a review of information currently available, external and internal facilities which can be drawn upon for analyses and the gathering of additional information, and the adequacy of such facilities.

INFORMATION CURRENTLY AVAILABLE

The Budget Document

The budget document contains general information about each proposed item of expenditure. Included in a budget description of a typical item is an introductory statement describing the purpose of the item, proposed language to be included in the pertinent appropriations bill, estimates of amount available for obligation with comparisons with the two fiscal years preceding the year for which the request is being made, an outline of "program and performance," a breakdown of "obligations by activities," "obligations by objects," and "analysis of expenditures" with comparisons with preceding years.

The budget, then, is the basic document available to Congress for consideration of appropriations. As noted in Chapter II, its value from an informational point of view is extremely limited, but it represents a good starting point.

Justification Sheets

The "justification sheets" are massive, mimeographed documents which break down most appropriation items, explaining in general how they are to be expended. The justification sheets are much more detailed than the budget document and represent the most comprehensive budgetary information prepared. Agency witnesses rely heavily on them during hearings for materials necessary to answer questions put by members of the Appropriations Subcommittees.

Justification sheets are available only to agency representatives, staff of the Bureau of the Budget, and members of Appropriations Subcommittees. They are not normally given, even on request, to Members of Congress who do not sit on appropriations committees. Members do not seek them very diligently anyway, since they consist of highly technical details presented in a framework of justification only. Nevertheless, justification sheets contain information necessary to any Member who is conscientious about expenditures issues. If it be said that the average Member is too busy for such concentrated study, it should be remembered that he may wish a staff assistant to review it for him so that his attention may be called to any unusual information his assistant is capable of pointing out.

Hearings Documents

The primary difficulties with hearings, as a source of information, have already been pointed out. These include the limitations of subcommittee members charged with bringing pertinent information to light, and the bias of witnesses, whose testimony is rarely objective and nearly always presented in a context of justification of the budget estimates or of even higher amounts. Despite these drawbacks, hearings represent the best single source of information on the details of appropriations requests that are generally available to all Members of Congress.

As an example of the types of information included in hearings documents, let us review that which was available in the 1952 hearings documents on the appropriations item "salaries and expenses, Department of State," which is the basic appropriation item for that Department since it provides funds for all the operations of the "State Department proper and the Foreign Service."[1]

Specific materials made available to Congress during the hearings for consideration of this item were as follows:

1. "Summary of requirements," which breaks down the item on the basis of departmental organization.
2. Summary of permanent positions by organization unit, a table which lists numbers of positions and salary costs by unit for the years 1951, 1952 and 1953 (the latter two being estimated). These, in turn, are broken down by subunits.
3. Various statements offered by departmental officials. These tend to concentrate on reasons for requesting new funds.

Questions by members of the House subcommittee were designed primarily to evoke explanations of proposals for increases. Discussions of breakdowns which involved figures the same as or lower than those for the previous fiscal year were perfunctory indeed.

The Senate subcommittee hearings consisted of 1,828 pages of testimony and exhibits, of which all but about 400 dealt with the Department of State.[2] Much of the basic materials presented during the Senate subcommittee hearings were those given before the House subcommittee. However, the greater length of the Senate hearings on the appropriations for the State Department (400 pages in the House, 1,400 in the Senate) gives a relevant comparison of the degree of thoroughness of program review on this particular item. About one-fourth of the Senate subcommittee hearings was devoted to gathering information about programs paid for by the "salaries and expenses" item (plus another one-sixth if we include material relating to loyalty programs and issues).

In reviewing the Senate hearings, one notes the heavy emphasis given not to expenditures as such but to administrative oversight of policies. This fact was evidenced by the amounts recommended by both subcommittee and full committee of the Senate.[3] After hundreds of pages of close questioning about various phases of different programs, the committee granted the Department an increase over the amount passed by the House of $1,392,306, although this was still $2,507,694 less than the budget request.

Thus the subcommittees can have made available to them all sorts of descriptions and itemized details—how many persons work in each administrative unit and the general purposes of each unit. It can get comparisons of employment and/or expenditures figures for prior years. It may also, of course, reduce the amount requested simply because it disagrees with an agency's purposes.

Assuming an agreement on basic policies involved in the State Department operations covered by the salaries and expenses item, Congress must rely principally on one of two theories: (a) our foreign relations are too important to risk any cuts, or (b) the Department can absorb nominal reductions without great harm to our foreign programs. Perhaps, in view of the executive prerogative in the sphere of international relations, this is as it should be. Yet if Congress had available objective analyses of the State Department's activities, with emphasis on what is being done and how much is proposed to be spent in relation to national objectives, that body might be able more nearly to assess the appropriateness of various amounts. On the one hand, it might be able to justify even more severe reductions than those proposed during the debates, but also, with such information, it might recognize that the full amounts requested should be granted in the interests of preserving or improving our relations with other nations.

In *The Purse and the Sword,* Elias Huzar quoted Representative Ben F. Jensen, Republican of Iowa, on the congressional lack of information upon which to pass judgment on spending requests. But Huzar pointed out that the real need went beyond even the lack of information. In discussing military appropriations, he said:

> Administrators usually have been ready to provide legislators with information about their work, even when it was unfavorable to them —if Congress insisted on it. . . .
> The subcommittee's chief problem is not one of getting data about appropriations and expenditures from independent sources, but of knowing for what to ask . . . and how to evaluate it.[4]

Thus the inadequacy of hearings implies no lack of willingness on the part of administrators to furnish any information the subcommittees may seek. The lack, rather, is the failure of the subcommittees even to ask significant questions and to evaluate data already available to them.

"Side Slips"

When an Appropriations Subcommittee, or full committee, meets to "mark up" a bill, each member receives memoranda known as "side slips." These are prepared by the staff and include for every item the most basic information relating to such items. This information is drawn from the budget document, justification sheets, hearings, and any other pertinent sources (such as special letters requesting data and various reports). Side slips may or may not be made available on request to Members of Congress generally, depending on the attitude of the subcommittee chairman.

The side slips show the agency concerned, the item, page references to the House bill and committee report and the Senate hearings, the amount of the estimate, the amount provided for the previous year, and the amount allowed by the House. In addition, the side slips contain amendments which have been requested and by whom they are sought, the pertinent passage from the House committee report, excerpts from the justification sheets, summary of estimates by activities, excerpts from the hearings, employment comparisons with previous years, and payments planned to be made above basic rates.

Side slips are thus the most succinct source of information available. Their value, however, depends upon the quality and completeness of the materials from which they are drawn.

Committee Reports

Appropriations Committee reports on appropriations bills contain what is considered to be the most important information about the pertinent appropriations items, combined with the committee's recommendations as to amounts and purposes. Committee reports are orginally drafted by the subcommittee staffs to include amounts voted by the subcommittee and statements of purpose and explanations written in accordance with subcommittee instructions. When the subcommittee orders the bill to be reported to the full committee, the report draft and the bill are reproduced in limited quantities as a "committee print" for the exclusive use of the members of the full committee. Occasionally, however, the "committee print" will be made available to the press corps, serving as a "press release" if the subcommittee desires that its action be made public in advance of full committee consideration.

The full committee may or may not change the amounts recommended and the statements included in the report. Whatever their final action, the report as modified is filed with the appropriate House of Congress, receives a number, and is printed in sufficient quantities to be available to any person seeking a copy.

Usually, House committee reports are more lengthy and detailed than those filed in the Senate since the Senate reports tend to concentrate on areas where their recommendations are different from those enacted by the House. These documents, along with floor statements by subcommittee chairmen, are the "justifications" of committee actions.

Other Sources of Information

In addition to the foregoing basic sources of information pertinent to appropriations matters, Members of Congress may draw upon a variety of other research materials. These other sources, which are either very sketchy or relate only to a specific area, include:

1. Agency reports, which set forth much information about specific programs and operations. General data may be obtained from agencies' annual reports, but special reports such as those prepared by the Corps of Engineers and the Bureau of Reclamation on specific construction projects are extremely valuable.
2. Special studies and reports prepared by such groups as the General Accounting Office, the Legislative Reference Service of the Library of Congress, other congressional committees, and special commissions. Such studies rarely relate directly to appropriations matters but are often helpful in their analysis of operating programs.
3. Published articles in the press and current periodicals, which are a mixed blessing. Often, in an attempt to make news or a political issue, such articles may be misleading, but alert newsmen can be

helpful to Members of Congress by uncovering tips or areas requiring study.

Early in 1952, Senator Robert Hendrickson, of New Jersey, introduced in the *Congressional Record* a news item from the *Newark Evening News* captioned "Seven Hundred and Fifty Dollars a Week Paid Plumber."[5] The story related to a contract let by the Atomic Energy Commission for construction work in Nevada. The Senator admonished the Members that if the facts in the article were true (and the agency did not refute them) it was high time that the Congress should start vigilantly to scrutinize all government contracts. The House Appropriations Subcommittee considering atomic energy appropriations was greatly disturbed by Senator Hendrickson's revelation, and ultimately recommended a proviso in the bill to prevent the use of cost-plus contracts, which were blamed for such laxity.

On the other hand, numerous disparaging articles about the Voice of America program were published in various newspapers during the period 1951–52. Specific charges were successfully refuted by the Department of State during the House Appropriations Subcommittee hearings in 1952, however, with the net effect being pretty much a waste of time.[6]

The preceding listing of information currently available to Congress for the consideration of appropriations matters consists entirely of published materials. Despite some limitations, these materials taken together may be about as complete a source of published data as necessary. Thus, the lack of congressional information lies mostly in the realm of securing more specific materials, implying an ability to pose pertinent questions to agency representatives (an ability currently lacking, according to Huzar), combined with better interpretations, evaluations, and analyses of existing materials.

External Facilities Currently Available

Let us turn now to facilities outside of Congress which are currently available for interpretation and analysis of spending issues. These would include the Bureau of the Budget and the executive agencies, the General Accounting Office, the Legislative Reference Service of the Library of Congress, and miscellaneous private groups and individuals.

The Bureau of the Budget and the Executive Agencies

As the central point of budget preparation, the Bureau of the Budget is considered as the central source of information to Congress on appropriations matters. Responsible for the final preparation of the budget document, the Bureau acts as an arm of the Executive, but is also in a position to provide information on the details and implications of expenditures requests to Members of Congress.

The value of the Bureau of the Budget as an indispensable tool of administrative direction employed by the President is widely recognized. It is probably the President's most effective weapon for bringing some semblance of order out of what starts out to be chaos. Moreover, the Bureau of the Budget is a tremendous aid to Congress in its search for information upon which to base its appropriations enactments. Yet if Congerss is to use independent judgment, it cannot rely exclusively on the Bureau of the Budget to furnish impartial information. For, as has been pointed out, when the Budget of the United States is presented to Congress by the President, so far as the Bureau is concerned, all decisions have been made. The budget document becomes the "President's budget" and, as such, must be defended and justified by the Bureau as well as explained.

In the first place, not only is the Bureau in the executive branch of the government; more important, it is in the Executive Office of the President. The formulation of the budget is an integral part of the formulation of the President's administrative policies. This process involves much pulling and hauling over both policies and judgments within the administration. When the process has reached completion, the budget document stands as a working agreement between the various agencies with virtually all money issues ironed out through the Bureau or the President, himself. To reopen the entire process before the congressional Appropriations Committees (although these committees often will ask an agency how much it originally sought for budget approval) is unthinkable. It would bog down Congress in considering appropriations, sinking it in a maze of contradictions and interagency rivalries. It could virtually destroy presidential leadership in the President's own bailiwick.

The administrative necessity of a unified budgetary presentation before Congress is the reason that Congress cannot depend on the Bureau or agency representatives for a critical analysis of the money requests. As we have said, these representatives can explain the requests to Congress, being very helpful, but if one of them were to tell Members of Congress that, in his judgment, certain items in the budget could be reduced, he would be flying in the face of presidential decisions to the contrary. This would lead to an atomization of presidential authority, producing chaos. Thus, to say that Congress cannot count on the Bureau for independent analyses is neither a criticism nor an indictment. It is mere statement of fact.

Then there are the agencies. If a Member of Congress wants to work for legislation favored by a particular agency, he will be immediately offered help in marshalling arguments, assuming he is interested in increasing the appropriations of that agency. But when he proposes to look into its appropriations with an eye to possible reductions, the reaction is somewhat less positive. Nevertheless, it is possible to get some information from the agencies which is useful if carefully checked and cross-examined.

The limitations on the value to Congress of interpretive materials furnished by the Bureau of the Budget and the executive agencies has been discussed in relation to their limitations during the hearings process and the usefulness of the hearings documents. The resulting dilemma facing Congress in its search for objective and critical comments has been discussed by Griffith:

> I well remember a characterization of government research I once heard in an address by Luther Gulick. He took us in imagination to a huge room whose walls were covered with files and pigeonholes labeled "Facts." In and out of the room came and went a continuous procession of men carrying sheets of paper. When the men came in, their sheets were blank, save for the conclusions. Diligent search would then be made among the files and pigeonholes for the facts which would add up to the preconceived conclusions. Such facts, when found, were duly entered, and, with the documents thus prepared to the satisfaction of the researcher, he would leave the room. This, said Gulick, was "government research"—of sorts, no doubt, but a characterization with a sufficient element of truth in it to evoke an appreciative response from his listeners.
>
> Conversely, those in Congress who held positions on issues other than those held by the executive found themselves severely limited both in inquiry and in debate. Leaks from dissenters within the executive, private research organizations, special interests—these were

hardly a match for the mass of facts and figures presented by an executive cloaked with the aura of the "public interest" and monolithic in its rejoinders to any criticism.[7]

Another weakness of congressional reliance on the agencies lies with the reluctance on the part of agency chiefs to change their minds once a position has been assumed. While prevalent in all walks of life and in all varieties of bureaucrat, this tendency is especially dangerous when found in the armed services. In this area of policy the mysteries of the technical combined with the further mysteries of necessary secrecy which surrounds so much that is basic to reaching a decision render Congress virtually powerless. Yet, as Griffith points out, the legislative body cannot and dare not delegate all responsibility in this area. The reliance of the French Chamber of Deputies upon the Maginot line because of the advice of its General Staff resulted in catastrophe. The real question is often not so much whether a particular agency expert is right or wrong on some matter but whether there are alternatives policies needing consideration along with the agency viewpoint.

Moreover, an agency chief normally recommends policies that involve expansion of his own staff and powers. This is not necessarily based on sinister or selfish motives of "empire building." A good administrator quite naturally will believe in the objectives of his agency. Thus, if he is given a large staff or greater powers, he feels this will enable him better to attain these objectives and do a better job. Of such tendencies among bureaucrats, Griffith has said:

> This is not itself an evil, provided he must justify his recommendations before a body commanding the same authoritative technical competence and one which, at the same time, has not vested interest in or drive toward such expansion. If the Congressional committee which, under the usages of our Constitution, has the primary responsibility to pass judgment on the request does not itself have in its own membership or in the alternative sources of information and analysis open to it a roughly comparable competence in the field in question, it is naturally a very considerable disadvantage in passing judgment on the request for greater staff or greater powers. The result may be as great an evil, if in blind resentment or perplexity a Congress rejects any and all such requests, as it is if a Congress is the unwitting dupe of the executive in granting them. The fact that Congress in practice has never become a prey to either of these extremes does not remove the danger of failing measurably short of

the best decision in a given instance through lack of mastery of its subject matter.[8]

The foregoing defects in reliance upon executive research, analysis, recommendations, and expertness have often caused Congress to doubt even apparently well-documented requests.

General Accounting Office

The major congressional agency available to Congress for help on expenditures matters is the General Accounting Office, headed by the Comptroller General. Created by the Budget and Accounting Act of 1921, this office is a part of the legislative branch of the government and is independent of executive domination. It audits and settles the accounts and claims of the government and advises and assists the Congress and the executive agencies on matters relating to expenditures.

The General Accounting Office maintains certain accounts of appropriations and personal ledger accounts with the fiscal officers who collect and disburse public funds. It uses those accounts, together with analyses of appropriations and other fiscal legislation, in the performance of its functions of approving warrants and settling the accounts of such officers. This procedure contributes to the enforcement by the General Accounting Office of the constitutional mandate that "no money shall be drawn from the Treasury, but in consequence of appropriations made by law." Mainly, through the Government-type audit, the General Accounting Office has collected and paid into the Treasury during the past few years hundreds of millions of dollars illegally or improperly paid out or withheld.

The Budget and Accounting Act directs the Comptroller General to investigate all matters relating to the receipt, disbursement, and application of public funds, and to make such investigations as are ordered by either Houses of Congress or any committee having jurisdiction over revenues, appropriations, or expenditures. A later statute requires the Comptroller General to examine all inactive and permanent appropriations on the books of the Government and all funds in the official custody of officers and employees of the United States in which the United States is financially concerned and for which no accounting is made to the General Accounting Office.

The investigative function of the General Accounting Office

goes beyond and supplements the audit and settlement procedures. It is intended to throw light on matters which may not be disclosed in audits. The work is geared to detecting fraud or irregularity hidden from the regular audit, and determining in general the propriety and effectiveness of the use of public funds and property and the adequacy of the accounting for such use.

Representatives of the General Accounting Office are regularly engaged in the inspection of offices, accounts, records, and practices of officers charged with the custody and use of public funds or property. They also investigate facts and information arising from those inspections, from the regular audit and settlement of accounts, and from outside sources. Responsible officers, including agency heads when appropriate and Congress when necessary, are advised of weaknesses, shortcomings, or irregularities; and proper corrective measures are suggested. Special investigations are made and aid furnished upon request of the Congress, either House, or the standing committees.

The Budget and Accounting Act requires the Comptroller General to make reports ordered by either House or any committee having jurisdiction over revenues, appropriations, or expenditures; and, through administrative examination and inspection of fiscal accounts and offices, to report on any expenditure or contract made in violation of law. Matters of financial concern to the United States, brought to light in the regular work of the General Accounting Office, are the subject of numerous reports by the Comptroller General on his own initiative. In 1951–52, the GAO submitted 47 comprehensive audit reports to Congress. It also made 685 reports to Congress and its committees and 3,500 replies to inquiries it received from individual Members of Congress.[9]

Section 206 of the Legislative Reorganization Act of 1946 directs the Comptroller General to make an expenditure analysis of each agency in the executive branch of the government in an effort to help Congress determine whether public funds have been economically and efficiently administered, and to report the results of his findings to the Committees on Appropriations, Government Operations and other appropriate legislative committees of the two Houses. However, up to the present time this has not been done because no appropriation has been made by Congress for the General Accounting Office to carry out this program.

The usefulness of the General Accounting Office to Congress would be greatly increased if Section 206 of the Reorganization Act were to be implemented with the necessary appropriations. Nevertheless, the General Accounting Office, through its constant contact with government operations in the process of investigation and the keeping of accounts, and in the issuance of its reports, is one of the congressional sources for "leads." The audit reports of the GAO are particularly valuable. Tips about examples of waste and extravagance as well as maladministration are constantly received by the committees. Many of these are investigated prior to the hearings or form the subject of questions at the time of any agency's appearance.

The Legislative Reference Service

The Legislative Reference Service of the Library of Congress was estabished in 1914 "to gather, classify, and make available, in translations, indexes, digests, compilations, and bulletins, and otherwise, data for or bearing upon legislations, and to render such data serviceable to Congress and committees and Members thereof."[10] The Service was greatly strengthened by the Legislative Reorganization Act of 1946, which permitted the hiring of twenty "senior specialists" at the highest, nonsupervisory Civil Service grades. There has been considerable expansion of the use of the Service since World War II. Legislators ask the Service for memoranda and reports, drafts of speeches and articles, graphs, bibliographies, consultation, and advice. It has become the principal general research arm of the Congress.

Under the leadership of Dr. Ernest S. Griffith, Director, from 1940 to 1958, the Legislative Reference Service developed a highly competent staff of some 160 lawyers, political scientists, economists, and other researchers and analysts. The Service is an invaluable aid to Congress in providing trained experts on virtually all phases of government operations.

The Legislative Reference Service has had experts in selected fields who, when given specific assignments, have provided valuable material. One such person, Mr. Charles Curran, was formerly an engineer with experience in both the Corps of Engineers and the Bureau of the Budget and thus brought to the Service a wealth of information about various federal construction programs. When either legislative or appropriations bills dealing with such programs came before Congress, his services were extremely valuable. At a Congressman's request, he was capable of reviewing and analyzing the proposals, developing the nature of each on the basis of a familiarity with the subject matter combined with knowledge of how to obtain pertinent information. The material he furnished did not contain policy judgments as such, but it was sufficient for a variety of judgments to be based on it, depending on what policies the Member was seeking.

It has been the policy of the Service to make its staff available to various congressional committees, and those staff members who become valuable to individual Members often become unavailable to the Service. Mr. Curran, for example, was first loaned to a subcommittee of the House Public Works Committee and later assisted the second Hoover Commission. Another example is Dr. Francis Wilcox, formerly with the Service, who became Staff Director of the Senate Foreign Relations Committee and later Assistant Secretary of State.

The limitations on the value of the Service to Congress in studying expenditure requests lie primarily with the nature of the Service. It responds to congressional requests, and this function is hampered unless Members know what questions to ask and the significance of the replies. Unlike The General Accounting Office, which must follow the operations of all government agencies, the Legislative Reference staff normally does work only on subjects where congressional requests have been made.

Nongovernment Facilities

The principal sources of nongovernment facilities available to Congress are the economic and/or political organizations. Such organizations are concerned with particular phases of federal programs from an economic or political point of view and desire to help Members of Congress when their efforts parallel those of the organizations.

Foremost among such nongovernment sources are the national party committees. Both Democratic and Republican National Committees maintain research and public relations arms, developing data for the use of their members. The committee of the party in control of the Administration will naturally develop materials favorable to the President's program, while that of the party out of power will seek out vulnerable spots for attack.

Private economic and political groups operate in much the same manner, but the emphasis is usually on specific policy areas rather than party lines. Every major farm, labor, and business lobby supports a research division and these tend to be staffed with well-paid, capable personnel. This is also true of the big trade and professional associations and groups organized around specific programs such as the National Rural Electric Association, the Savings and Loan Leagues, and the National Congress of Rivers and Harbors. None of these groups is unbiased, of course, but they serve the two-fold function of representing voters and providing information in competitive fields.

There are other, less formal sources of information which can be used by Members of Congress. Letters from private individuals can sometimes furnish leads to waste. Often, career government employees, feeling that it is their duty to do so, will privately disclose additional information qualifying that presented by the agencies. Of course, if a Member makes use of such information, he must carefully refrain from mentioning its source to prevent possible reprisals from the superiors of the employees. Moreover, a Member of Congress can make use of such "informers" only by cross-checking his information. He must guard against being misled by a disgruntled employee who seeks to discredit an agency for personal reasons.

These, then, are the congressional sources for interpretive and analytical data relating to the materials provided by the executive branch. None of them may be said to be unbiased, with the exceptions of the General Accounting Office, Legislative Reference Service, and an occasional private citizen. All are limited in that they do not make continuing analyses in an organized fashion as does the Bureau of the Budget. And as we have shown, Congress cannot rely on the Bureau for objective evaluation of expenditures issues.

INTERNAL FACILITIES—CONGRESSIONAL STAFFING

The staff personnel attached to individual Members and to the Committees represent the plane of the smallest diameter in the funnel of information to Congress. This diameter, once so small as to provide Members with only a trickle of knowledge, has steadily grown since the enactment of the Legislative Reorganization Act of 1946. Many informed persons, including some who serve on congressional staffs, feel that a further general enlargement could possibly result in a funnel mouth so wide as to cause a deluge of information impossible to absorb. The problem here is not one of quantity; rather, the difficulties lie with the quality of knowledge flowing in at the other end of the funnel.

In spite of the general picture painted above, there are certain exceptions which should be noted. The House of Representatives exercises responsibilities equal to the Senate. The fact that House Members may represent smaller districts than Senators or that there are more of them does not detract from the equal division of responsibility between the two Houses of Congress. Thus Representatives should be enabled to employ a topnotch research assistant as well as Senators, and House committees need to hire competent staff in numbers on a par with those in the Senate.

Appropriations Committee Staffs

A chairmanship of an Appropriations Subcommittee which takes primary responsibility for a large area of appropriations is tantamount to a chairmanship of a standing committee. Yet such subcommittees are given staffs equivalent to other subcommittees, usually one or, at most, two professional staff assistants. Discussing the Defense Appropriation Bill enacted in 1951, Senator Douglas wrote:

> I shall never forget my gasp of surprise when I discovered that the Senate Appropriations Committee had only one professional staff man to help evaluate a $61-billion appropriation bill for the Department of Defense. It would be difficult to imagine one man even keeping up with the mechanics of such a measure.[11]

During the 1952 House debates on the Defense appropriation, Representative Vursell of Illinois argued that the House committee had need of a larger investigative staff and other assistance so that

> the Congress could legislate in the light instead of legislating in the dark as we too often are compelled to do because our committees do not have sufficient staffs to determine the funds necessary, and a sufficient staff of investigators to constantly watch and check on the spending of this money to prevent waste.[12]

On the Senate side, during the same year, the debates on the Civil Functions appropriation evoked a remark by Senator Styles

Bridges of New Hampshire that "the Committee on Appropriations operates under very decided handicaps, with a lack of sufficient staff and a lack of opportunity for proper investigation."[13] Interestingly enough, Senator Bridges became Chairman of the Senate Appropriations Committee the following year, with no substantial changes in the makeup or size of the committee's staff.

Actually, both Appropriations Committees could probably employ as large a staff as they desired, but despite some growth in recent years, two factors tend to keep down the size. First, the committees tend to feel that they must set an example of austerity for other committees and government agencies. This reasoning may be self-defeating as in the case of a similar policy adopted by Charles G. Dawes, the first Director of the Bureau of the Budget, for *economy on overhead* (and that appears to be the historic watchword of the Appropriations Committees) would seem to be better achieved by careful analysis of the requests rather than the mere setting of an example. Second, Congress is not equipped to supervise a large bureaucracy directly, and some Congressmen fear losing control of policy by staff getting out of hand. Members must concern themselves with such a broad area of policy that day-to-day supervision of a large research operation would probably fail so miserably that some policies might be furthered by the staff without Members having sufficient understanding of the actions taken in their names.

As to their staffs, the Appropriations Committees and Members of Congress, too, must steer a course between Scylla and Charybdis—between inadequate help and an unwieldy bureaucracy. For this reason, flat recommendations for larger staffs fall short of the mark. Only the Members can decide what is best for them in this regard. However, one course which Members might consider would be to recognize that an Appropriations Subcommittee's responsibilities are usually not so much less than those of a full standing committee, and that a staffing might be arranged accordingly.

The Legislative Reorganization Act of 1946 permits each standing committee of Congress to appoint, by a majority vote of the committee, as many as four professional staff members, in addition to clerical staffs, with salaries currently as high as $16,300. Since 1946, professional staffs of congressional committees have grown considerably, even beyond the Act's limitations, by special resolutions.

Referring to the impact of the Legislative Reorganization Act as it affected the committees, Griffith has stated that it has introduced a " 'third force' of experts, usually designed as a corrective to the bias of the special interests and to any shortcomings in the substantive recommendations of the executive" and that it probably reversed a trend of "dominance of the bureaucracy over the legislative branch through the former's near-monopoly . . . of technical . . . competence. . . ."[14]

Opinion of informed observers bears out Griffith's statement on the improvement of legislative committee staffs but not on the sufficiency of Appropriations Committee staffs. If one takes into account the difficulties of supervising an excessively large staff, however, it would appear that if Appropriations Subcommittees were to be staffed as standing committees, the potential of the staff as an aid to subcommittee members would be more nearly reached.

The role of the committee staff, in considering congressional staff aids, must be borne in mind. They rarely work with individual Members who are not on the committee they serve, except through formal requests of the committee chairman. Their primary concern is to help their particular committee members, especially the chairman, since it is here that allegiance is owed. Far from helping individuals, they are more often called upon, during floor debate, to furnish material designed to combat proposals made by nonmembers. This is a proper function, of course. Individual Members should rely on their personal staffs or other sources of assistance.

Personal Staffs

Normally, an outside staff cannot make policy evaluations; a Member can use his personal staff for this. A personal staff assistant, dealing with only one Member, learns his employer's temperament and philosophy through working together. Thus a personal assistant can develop programs for his principal to accept, modify, or reject. In order for this to be possible, however, the Member must develop knowledge of his assistant's capabilities and limitations as well as his orientation (or biases). This he must do if he is to cover a large legislative waterfront, since time will not permit him to develop everything himself. Nevertheless, like his employer, the personal assistant cannot be an expert in all fields of expenditure.

Senators are given allowances sufficient to hire staffs of from ten, for those from smaller States, to twenty for those representing the larger States. Representatives are granted a staff allowance to permit them to employ between four and nine persons, depending upon the size of the salaries paid.

Legislative work, however, accounts for only a part of the time of a Member of Congress. Among other things, he also fulfills speaking engagements, writes articles, campaigns for his fellow party members, engages in political negotiations in State politics, clears and helps to fill federal patronage positions, and serves as federal "alderman" to his constituents in helping them to disentangle themselves when they get ensnarled in the complexities of federal administrative programs and need guidance on such matters as Social Security problems, veteran's benefits, and immigration of friends and relatives.

Thus Members are responsible for a sizeable staff operation on matters other than legislation. The size of the total work load limits the degree to which they can assign staff to legislative work —normally only one in the case of Representatives and from one to three in the case of Senators. As in the case of the committees, however, a Member is not equipped to direct large staff operations. Current personal staff facilities are probably adequate or near-adequate. Again, the problem is at the large, rather than the small end of the information funnel.

The Need for More Adequate Facilities

The information and facilities available to Members of Congress is astounding. These include the budget document, justification sheets, hearings documents, side slips (committee staff memoranda), committee reports, agency reports, special studies, and published articles in the press and current periodicals. The agencies treat congressional requests for data or assistance with top priority. The Library of Congress, the best library in the world, provides speedy service, and the Legislative Reference Service of the Library will carry out almost any research requested by any Member, no matter how petty or how large (within the bounds of persuasive reason). Committee and personal staffs assist Members with advice, analyses, and the processsing of constituents' requests. The Office of the Legislative Counsel, a bill-drafting service available in both Houses of Congress, drafts measures incorporating any policy a Member may wish to pursue. Page boys and riding pages run errands for him.

In short, the Member of Congress can carry out his tasks with adequate assistance in most areas, but there are notable exceptions. Among these is that of the gathering, analysis, and organization of factual data necessary for rendering his independent judgment and offering and defending proposals dealing with money requests. The reasons for this lack lie not so much with the Member's general facilities as with the nature and scope of spending matters and the lack of specific facilities for dealing with them.

Griffith has hit at the core of the problems facing Congress on spending matters:

> The appropriating process is almost the only point in the Congressional agenda at which the program of the government passes in view in its totality. Here legislative intent can be enhanced and promoted; here also it can be hampered or strangled altogether.... The pressure groups beat upon the committee doors. The executive masses its persuasion and its coerciveness, its facts and its subterfuges. The Appropriations Committees have the largest memberships and the largest staffs of any of the standing committees. Their tasks are incomparably the most difficult.
>
> Some of these difficulties are patent. The sheer size of the total budget is one.... If appropriations are to be considered in detail, there are not days, weeks, and months enough to cover the ground. If it is in lump sums, who is to judge whether the amount is too much or too little to attain the end?... Whole sections of expenditure, especially in the military, are shrouded in secrecy and must be accepted largely on faith.... The approach employed by the executive retains the fiction of the equal importance of all items in the estimates, and what would be enormously valuable assistance from the Bureau of the Budget or the agency itself, in assessing priorities, is not forthcoming.[15]

Griffith's statement is substantiated in page after page of the *Congressional Record*, but for our purposes two sample instances should suffice. During the debate on the Post Office Department Appropriation Bill in 1952, it was not an individual Member but the subcommittee chairman who stated: "Frankly, there is not very much that can be done about the Post Office Department appropriation."[16] One item in that bill, postal operations, accounted for nearly one-fourth of all civilian operating expenditures of the entire Federal Government. Virtually all information about it came from the Department concerned with no adequate means available

PART I. *Preparations for Control*

to cross-check any of it. The appropriation was so large and complex that without better analytical data it was not understood by Congress.

In the same year, during the debate on the Defense Department appropriation, another Member (Werdel) complained that "we should have something besides the prepared manuscripts from the Pentagon in order to justify a favorable vote on this bill for this amount of money."[17]

Serious questions naturally arise over the fact that Congress lacks the facilities for controlling appropriations. The problem goes beyond lack of control over expenditures, however, because an absence of facilities does not lead Congress to abandon its attempts to control. And these attempts, necessarily made without proper knowledge of their consequences, quite often play havoc with the existing degree of order and effectiveness of the agencies' operations.

PART II

Techniques of Control

Chapter **4**

Playing it Safe
Legislative Conservatism

Congressional attempts to control federal spending take a great variety of forms. Effective or not, all represent efforts by Members to carry out their functions as they conceive them, but Congress enacts very few appropriations bills with any high degree of knowledge of the real consequences of its actions.

The techniques devised by Congress to control spending are numerous but can be classified as to their general nature into six main categories:

1. *Appeals to legislative conservatism:* appeals to precedent, resisting proposals to increase or lower expenditures as compared with amounts enacted for previous years.
2. *Meat-axe cuts:* general across-the-board reductions or arbitrary cuts inflicted to force lower expenditures and more economic operations.
3. *Attacks on overhead:* cuts aimed at operating overhead while preserving the program, or legislative riders designed to force savings in administrative costs.
4. *Work for local interests:* efforts to make the general interest coincide with local interests, especially on construction items.
5. *Legerdemain:* use of bookkeeping methods to produce the appearance rather than the substance of economy.
6. *Legislative standards:* use of standards in authorizing legislation in order to ascertain the results of appropriations actions.

More than one of the techniques listed above may be joined together. In 1952, for example, Senator Homer Ferguson of Michigan, a Republican member of the Appropriations Committee, successfully proposed an amendment to nearly all appropriations bills which provided that funds for personnel could not exceed 90 per-

cent of the amounts budgeted for that purpose. The effect was a
10 percent reduction in funds requested for the payment of salaries
to employees of the agencies. It probably succeeded because it contained the three most popular methods of applying economy. First,
it held funds for personnel more closely to the amounts provided
for the previous year—legislative conservatism; second, it cut in
a straight line across many agencies—the meat axe; and third, it
made reductions in operating expenses applying only to personnel
—an attack on overhead.

In this chapter, we shall consider congressional resistance to increases or reductions in amounts enacted for prior years, based on
the principle of legislative conservatism, and see how this method
affects an over-all budget and two specific appropriation items for
international programs. The other general methods will be discussed in following chapters.

Legislative Conservatism

Joseph P. Chamberlin has stated that

> in a legislature, it is normally up to the proponent of legislation to
> establish his case . . . in the main such a body is conservative and slow
> to move, except where a case, already strong, is supported by a pre-
> ponderant public opinion on the question at issue.[1]

Another scholar, George B. Galloway, has stated that in Congress

> The almost universal legislative attitude is that the burden of proof
> is on the advocate. Congress is disinclined to make an important
> change of law where there is serious opposition to such change even
> though a majority . . . favor the proponents. A legislature is inclined
> to be mildly conservative about changing the rules under which
> people are living. It must be satisfied, not only that the change is
> desirable, but that the great majority of the people want it.[2]

The conservative attitude which Congress takes with respect to
new legislation operates also in the case of departures from established appropriations schedules, although tempered to a considerable degree by the general desire for economy. As a result, the
agency which seeks the same amounts it has spent in prior years
will fare better than one which attempts to expand its operations.
Not only is the burden of proof on those agencies seeking increases;
the same burden is on those persons seeking reductions below prior
year appropriations for agencies resisting such cutbacks.

Legislative conservatism leads subcommittee members to devote most of their questions during the hearing to items where the requests are higher than in previous years. Persuasive reasoning must usually be given by the agencies requesting increases; if not, the committee recommendations are likely to cut back the requests to the level of preceding years. Moreover, the subcommittees are critical of agencies which depart in their justification from comparison with previous years, even if such comparisions are not practicable. A 1952 document of the House Armed Services Appropriations Subcommittee, for example, commented:

> Justifications submitted in support of the budget requests were, in many respects, very unsatisfactory.... The manner in which the budgetary laws are being interpreted in the departments does not appear to lend itself readily to providing the type of information the committee and the Congress has received for many years and which must be available if proper consideration and review of budget requests are to be made.[3]

In this case, as in others, the main device for checking on proposed programs was to attempt a comparison with the number of personnel assigned in past years with the number estimated as being required to perform a certain project or function.

During the House floor debate on the same measure, Representative John Taber, Republican of New York, gave expression again to the major criteria by which Congress attempts to control the purse strings: "Frankly, this whole military picture needs revamping from a budget standpoint so that these people will be made to justify the items in some intelligent way so that we can compare their operations with *what has gone before*."[4] (Italics are mine.)

Legislative conservatism is not restricted to agency requests, however. In the 1952 House debate on the Civil Functions Appropriation Bill, four amendments, all in the interest of adding funds for additional construction, were rejected after a statement by a member of the subcommittee, Rep. Louis C. Rabaut of Michigan, that:

> Our committee reduction was achieved by allowing the same amount as in 1952. Anybody that gets the same amount for 1953 that they got in 1952, with the war effort and the defense program and the tremendous expenditures going on in this country, is doing pretty well.[5]

The effectiveness of legislative conservatism is not restricted to that employed by subcommittee members in defense of their recommendations. The same principle can be used successfully to oppose such recommendations. This was done by Senator Francis Case, Republican of South Dakota, during the 1952 Senate debate on the State, Justice, Commerce, and Judiciary Appropriation Bill, when the Senate passed his amendment making reductions in the funds for Foreign Service personnel of the Department of State.[6] The Department had sought an increase in these funds which it justified because of the proposed establishment of a new embassy in Tokyo, and the Senate Appropriations Committee had recommended that a sizable portion of the increased request be granted.

Senator Case's arguments for denying the increase appealed to the principle of legislative conservatism, citing a comparison of budgeted figures with those of previous years. He did not oppose the establishment of an embassy in Tokya, but he pointed out that the proposed size of it, 214 Americans and 257 non-Americans, compared with a total of 82 American employees in 1941—a proposed increase of nearly 300 percent—seemed grossly excessive. By letters to the State Department, he secured similar comparisons for a variety of important countries, discovering that Foreign Service officers had greatly increased in number between 1940 and 1952. The same was true of personnel of the State Department at selected posts.

The committee recommendation was defended by the chairman of the subcommittee, whose only defense in the face of these prior year comparisons was that staff should be available in the numbers recommended—otherwise, Congress would "cripple the Service which has been established by statute."[7] Senator Case's amendment carried by a vote of 46 to 36.

Although defense requirements caused some violent fluctuations in the total amounts Congress appropriated for 1953 as compared with 1952, a comparison of the amounts enacted for those two years in six appropriation bills substantiates the tendency towards legislative conservatism. Such a comparison is made in Table 4, which shows that despite healthy increases in the amounts requested for 1953, the final enactments were very close to those passed for the previous year. Most requested increases were not granted, but neither did the amounts approved represent any substantial reductions below the amounts passed for 1952.

PART II. *Techniques of Control*

Table 4

COMPARISON OF 1953 BUDGET REQUESTS, AMOUNTS
APPROPRIATED, AND AMOUNTS APPROPRIATED
FOR 1952: SELECTED BILLS

(in millions)

Bill	Budget Request for 1953	Amount Appropriated for 1953	Amount Appropriated for 1952
Independent Offices..............	$6,982	$6,272	$6,162
Interior........................	632	541	512
Civil Functions..................	713	584	597
State, Justice, Commerce and the Judiciary......................	1,243	1,016	1,042
Legislative Branch...............	86	77	74
Agriculture.....................	932	838	803

Source: Columns 2 and 3 from Cong. Rec., 82d Cong., 2d Sess. (1952), (Daily ed.) July 22, 1952, p. D718; column 4 from Cong. Rec., 82d Cong., 1st Sess. (1951), XCVII, Part 15, A6673.

There is a reason for legislative conservatism, especially on appropriations. Congress feels safer in holding the line on appropriations enacted in previous years because of a lack of certainty about the consequences of any changes. A proposal to cut or to increase must attract wide popular support or have firm justification to succeed. Congress, generally, has not the information or the facilities to feel confident of sudden changes, one way or the other.

INTERNATIONAL PROGRAMS

Appropriations items for international programs are especially subject to the influence of legislative conservatism, for these programs are unique in several respects. In the first place, the purposes behind our foreign relations are basically political: to strengthen our national security by maintaining friendly relations with other nations, to avoid frictions leading to war, if possible, or to build up a strong array of allies if war should come; and also to make possible greater economic opportunities in foreign trade.

Foreign relations involve differences of opinion on methods for agreed-upon policies, but they also involve controversy in the basic policies. These basic policy differences tend to overshadow methods, and debates over appropriations items, in accordance with recommendations of many students, tend to concentrate on broad policy issues rather than on the details of administration. However, the difficulty of understanding the effectiveness of methods also accounts for congressional tendencies to debate only the broad policy issues and rely heavily on the principle of legislative conservatism in the enactment of appropriations for such programs.

Let us consider the appropriation item in the 1953 budget for international information and educational activities, an activity of the Department of State. The Budget request for this item was $133,300,000,[8] whereas the appropriation for the previous year had been $86,600,000.[9] The House committee report recommended $111,100,000 for this activity but criticized the information programs for the practice of asking for increased funds year after year to expand operations.[10] In general, however, the cuts in the budget requests made on individual items were not substantial.

Rep. Charles Brownson of Indiana, appealing to legislative conservatism, offered an amendment to cut the amount from $111,100,000 to $86,600,000, the same figure as had been appropriated for the previous year. He indicated that he was not attacking the purpose of the program, but that such questions as: "Is the thing being done sensibly?" and "Are we getting our money's worth?" ought to be satisfactorily answered before granting increases over the amounts appropriated for the previous years. These questions were constantly reiterated in the form of criticisms of the administration of the program and its effectiveness (as in its alleged failure to influence a growing Communist vote in France and Italy), and of the tendency to further expansion and "empire building." Opponents of the amendment to cut the appropriation pointed to Russia's huge expenditures in the field of propaganda and to comparatively small investment involved in this type of cold-war weapon compared with the price of a single battleship. Nevertheless, the House apparently felt that it was safe to cut so long as the amounts provided were the same as that for the preceding year. Legislative conservatism won the day, and the amendment cutting the appropriation to $86,600,000 was accepted by the House.[11]

In its report, the Senate committee stated its belief that the amount allowed by the House, $86,600,000, would be adequate to pursue the same program as during the preceding year.[12] The debate in the Senate was cursory. No attempt was made to restore the cuts.

CONCLUSIONS

Let us consider the information Congress had before it to review this item. A source of "facts" quoted by some Members was press reports and comments. Disparaging articles by Willard Edwards, which appeared in the Washington *Times-Herald*, were inserted in the *Congressional Record*.[13] So severely critical were six articles by a former State Department employee, Frank Stout, which appeared in the Scranton (Pennsylvania) *Tribune*, that the Department felt the necessity to refute them point by point at the hearings. These charges were repeated later in newspaper columns written by Fulton Lewis, Jr.[14] Also at Congress' disposal was a report submitted to G. W. Lawson, Jr., Chief of the International Activities Branch of the Bureau of the Budget. Made by two Congressmen who had taken a fact-finding trip to eight Western European countries, it reflected the chief over-all problems of the program. Strangely, the report does not appear in the subcommittee hearings but was brought to the House's attention during debates on the floor.[15]

From the debate in the House it is possible to detect a number of other sources utilized by Members to judge appropriations. Rep. Charles Brownson of Indiana quoted a veteran Foreign Service officer's personal objections to the large number of young Ph.D.'s sent abroad as information officers. Several Members who arose to criticize the agency and to support cutbacks referred to their own trips abroad. Rep. O. K. Armstrong of Missouri asserted that during several trips to Europe and the Far East, he asked the question: "What is the greatest weakness of the Voice of America and the Information and Education Service of the United States?" and received answers from "outstanding citizens of foreign countries" and a "responsible spokesman for a government in Europe." Another Member, Rep. George Bender of Ohio said: "We were only there twelve days, but we were there long enough to listen to the Voice of America and to the Voice of Russia." Rep. Harris Ellsworth of Washington stated he had been in Europe twice the preceding fall, learning there:

... absolutely unmistakably that the Radio Free Europe which has been sponsored by voluntary contributions is doing a terrific job, of which the Kremlin is frightened.... I could find nowhere evidence that the Russians were concerned with what the Voice of America was doing.[16]

Yet in the House committee hearings there was notable evidence that Russia was concerned about VOA broadcasts; State Department officials related the difficulties of the Voice with Russian jamming.[17]

But the primary body of information comes to Congress through Senate and House committee hearings. Here, the staff of the agency concerned justified their requests. Obviously, through devotion to their own cause, their presentation was made in terms favorable to their petition, and yet because of their participitation in the agency's activities, they were most qualified to discuss its requirements. This resulted in congressional dependence for facts on an advocate rather than an impartial analyst.

Although a substantial cut had been made, the hearings of the subcommittees do not reveal the line of reasoning which led it to make the reductions other than merely to hold funds to the 1952 level. The subcomittees were presented by the Department with summaries and tables detailing progress made in radio facility construction and itemizing past and future expenditures. However, they had no time to examine these statements prior to the hearings. At one point Rep. Prince Preston of Georgia commented, "I could hardly be prepared to ask an intelligent question." More basic than the lack of time to examine the Department's prepared exhibits was the fact that the appropriation involved technical aspects about which the subcommittees could not be expected to judge. Mr. Preston, frankly stated:

> When it comes to dealing with the ring plan and its justification, we are unqualified to pass on this technical field. We can simply say "yes" or "no" and give you the go ahead sign to expand the program and to create these facilities which we hope will make the program more effective.[18]

Congress' reliance upon newspaper articles, quick trips abroad, and hearsay evidence to counterbalance the enthusiastic claims of the petitioning agency undoubtedly caused frustrations for both the executive department, which sincerely wanted to do its job well, and Congress, which had to balance the double-edged knife of wanting to see the job well done, but in the most economic way. The frustrations of Congress caused that body, in its collective judgment, to rely on the principle of legislative conservatism and hold the appropriated amounts to the same level as had been enacted for the previous year.

The hearings and debates on the Voice of America appropriation would seem to be adequate in the opinion of those who feel that Congress should restrict itself to general policy considerations and avoid details. Certainly Congress acted as a "sounding board," ventilated the issues, and made vocal the criticisms of the "practical" men of political affairs.

Yet one must consider that if Congress had available objective analyses of the activities of the Voice of America, with emphasis on what was being done and what was proposed to be done in relation to national objectives, it might have been able to nearly to assess the appropriateness of the increased amounts requested. On the one hand, it might have been able to justify reductions even below the amounts approved for the previous year, but also, with such information, it might have recognized that no lowering of the amounts requested should have been carried out in the interests of preserving or improving our relationships with other nations.

Thus if our goal is to seek to permit Congress to exercise its spending power with a maximum of knowledge about the consequences of such exercise of power, the technique of legislative conservatism is not the answer. Certainly Congress needs better analytical tools than it had available during the consideration of the appropriation for the Voice of America.

Chapter **5**

The "Meat Axe"

Members of Congress who try to cut appropriations on individual items usually find themselves blocked by tendencies towards legislative conservatism and also by avid proponents of the specific programs affected. In order to avoid the onus of singling out individual agencies, many have tried the meat-axe method of spending reductions. An "across-the-board" cut, which pares all agency requests by the same percentage, is called a meat axe because it cuts in a straight line across a large area, as does a meat axe. The term is one of opprobrium because such a reduction hurts the efficient agencies to the same degree as the inefficient, and necessary programs suffer to the same extent as all others. The term is also applied to any reduction proposed for which the consequences, other than the money reductions, are not ascertained.

The meat axe is a favorite device for those seeking economies without regard to their effects on government operations. As Senator Paul Douglas of Illinois has stated, "The meat axe is easy. Just raise it above your head and come down on the bureaus with a resounding whack."[1] Congress adopts many such proposals because, in the absence of specific information as to where reductions might be applied more reasonably, there appear to be no other alternatives to economy.

The across-the-board and the arbitrary item reductions have, in a spirit of congressional "reasonableness," been combined in the form of an over-all lump-sum reduction to be allocated by the President or the Bureau of the Budget. Of the over-all cut on a percentage or lump-sum basis, Griffith has said:

This type has been gaining favor of late, in part as the response of a frustrated Congress to extreme difficulties involved in obtaining substantial economies by the alternative channel of the detailed consideration of a budget so increased in size as to be virtually past comprehension. On the other hand, this method has been severely attacked as constituting the virtual abdication of Congress of its appropriating responsibilities because, in effect, it restores discretionary spending to the Executive. . . .[2]

RELINQUISHING CONTROL TO THE EXECUTIVE

The over-all approach, from the standpoint of Congress, also involves difficulties because of its effects on policies. Giving the President or department heads blanket authority to allocate reductions could result in drastic cuts in areas where Congress would object and no cuts at all in programs which Congress felt should be reduced. The meat-axe cut is thus a method of wielding congressional power without congressional control. Moreover, administrative allocations of reductions could prove a source of political embarrassment to Congress, for the administrators could use their authority to pare funds for popular programs, blaming Congress on the need for such unpopular actions. Of course, Members of Congress could, in turn, take credit for the saving but blame the administrators for the actual reductions, leading to a mutual escape from responsibility.

Delegation of authority to the President to reduce appropriations was given by Congress in the Bridges-Byrd amendment to the General Appropriation Act, 1951. Section 1214 of the Act made reductions in appropriations in the amount of not less than $550,000,000, which was to be apportioned by the Director of the Bureau of the Budget. These reductions were to be made without impairing national defense. The Director of the Bureau ultimately made reductions of $572,729,925, which he applied to some 150 separate appropriations items (there were, roughly, 350 items in the bill).[3] Table 5 lists 17 individual item reductions in excess of $5,000,000. Of the 150 items reduced, these 17 accounted for $509,300,000 of the $572,700,000 total reduction, A glance at the list shows that virtually all of the 17 major reductions were made in popular programs. It would be unfair to say that the Bureau of the Budget made its major cuts in popular areas in order to embarass Members of Congress. The Korean war had broken out, and the reductions were concentrated on public works, a field generally considered to be a proper place for cutbacks during periods

Table 5

ITEM REDUCTIONS OF OVER $5,000,000 IN APPROPRIATIONS,
CONTRACT AUTHORIZATIONS, AND AUTHORIZATIONS
TO BORROW FROM THE TREASURY, FISCAL YEAR
1951, UNDER PROVISIONS OF SECTION 1214 OF
THE GENERAL APPROPRIATION ACT, 1951

Appropriation Item Reduced	Amount of Reduction (*Millions*)	Amount of Budget Requests (*Millions*)
Production and Marketing Administration, Conservation and Use of Agricultural Resources	$26.0	$285.0
Acreage Allotments and Marketing Quotas	9.2	34.0
Rural Electrification, Loan Authority	85.5	450.0
Farmers Home Administration, Loan Authority	24.5	160.0
Federal Aid Airport Program	15.5	88.0
Maintenance and Improvement of River and Harbor Works	15.8	240.7
Flood Control, General	27.3	478.4
Flood Control, Mississippi River	5.0	72.0
Government and Relief in Occupied Areas	50.0	320.0
General Services Administration, Public Buildings Outside of D.C.	21.0	28.0
Veterans Administration, Hospitals	10.0	887.8
Advance Planning of Non-Federal Public Works	15.0	40.0
Bureau of Reclamation, Construction	53.2	326.0
Bureau of Employment Security, Grants to the States	6.4	171.0
Public Health Services, Hospital Construction	75.0	150.0
Railroad Retirement Board, Railroad Retirement Account	19.8	594.0
Foreign Economic Cooperation	50.0	2,657.7
Total	$509.3	$6,982.6

Source: H. Doc. No. 182, 3d Cong., 1st Sess. (1951).

of defense buildup and war. Nevertheless, the effects of the reductions on policies which vitally concern Congress are clear.

CUTS TO FORCE ECONOMY

Meat-axe reductions on individual items and agencies, like the general cuts, are made because of a lack of adequate information and are often based on hearsay, hunches, and the fear of losing control of expenditures. Typical of this type of action was that taken by Congress on the money requests of the Department of Defense for the fiscal year 1953. Attempts made to exert congressional control over defense spending took the form of item reductions and the application of an expenditures ceiling on the amounts to be expended in a single fiscal year.

The difficulties facing Congress in considering appropriations relating to national defense result from their huge size and complexity, the secret nature of many of the expenditures, and the degree to which technical and defense policy questions are passed upon by Congress, essentially a nonexpert body. Despite these difficulties, however, Congress must pass on such estimates. Elias Huzar noted that one of the purposes of the Founding Fathers in giving Congress the power of the purse was to insure civilian control of the military forces. He stated, however, that "Congress has not had to try to protect the American people from dictatorship by refusing to appropriate funds for the Armies. . . . It has used its power vigorously for ends that are less dramatic but still valuable." He cited Justice Story's words that this power "constitutes a most useful and salutary check upon profusion and extravagance, as well as upon corrupt influence and public peculation."[4]

During the debates on the huge $52,000,000,000 request for Defense spending for the fiscal year 1953, there were many expressions by legislators that they had, to a great extent, and for a number of reasons, lost control of the purse. The several devices employed to hold or cut down appropriations and expenditures indicate the broad scope of this feeling. Not only were there huge unexpended funds available for military spending from past appropriations, but there were many charges and some specific examples of waste and extravagance in military expenditures. Countering this, however, was the advice from top military and civilian officials that a year of crisis over the Soviet threat was approaching.

In brief, after extensive hearings, the House Armed Services Appropriations Subcommittee reported the bill, recommending a cut in the President's estimates of about $4,250,000,000. In floor action, the House not only trimmed this figure further but also added a provision limiting military expenditures in fiscal 1953 to $46,000,000,000. These cuts and limitations brought sharp protests from the President and military leaders. The Senate Appropriations Subcommittee disregarded the complaints against the House cuts and reduced the figure somewhat further, but deleted the $46,000,000,000 spending limit.[5] Conferees on the bill agreed on an appropriation of $46,000,000,000 without the expenditures ceiling.

As is true of congressional action on civilian items, the most common attempts to control were really efforts to force economies by cuts in the requests. The House committee cut of about 10 percent was obviously made as an attempt to enforce "economy and efficiency" and as punishment for the reported waste and extravagance. This was frankly admitted in a committee document, which stated:

> ... a considerable portion of the 4.2 billion dollar reduction in the current bill has been made with the specific purpose in mind of enforcing a better job of military management and expenditure. Some way must be found to shock the Department of Defense from top to bottom into the full realization that Congress and the American people will not tolerate waste in money and manpower.[6]

Many members seemed certain that widespread military waste and extravagance existed, although it was difficult to pin down. They apparently felt that the only way they could combat it was to cut it arbitrarily. In the words of Rep. James C. Davis of Georgia:

> If this committee, having given the study which it has to this bill, over all these weeks, has not been able to put its finger on that waste and extravagance so as to cut it out, what other method is there of cutting it out than except to reduce this bill?[7]

The Senate subcommittee recommended that the "aircraft and related procurement" item be cut by $600,000,000, but stated in its report that it did not intend to curtail the 143-group Air Force program, the cut being "designed solely to effect an economy in the procurement of the component spares and spare parts."[8]

Senators were advised by the Air Force that cuts in the requests would "knock out about 700 aircraft from the program," set back the program 9 to 12 months, and "play hob with current aircraft production schedules. . . ."[9] The Senate did not heed the advice of Air Force officials in this case, and approved the recommendations of its subcommittee.

Both successful and unsuccessful efforts to force economies by simple reductions in the requests were made. No doubt those which succeeded did reduce the amount of spending authority that was to be made available to the Department of Defense. But it is highly doubtful that the true consequences of these actions were known to Members of Congress, who swung the axe because the agencies opposed virtually all proposals for reductions with equal vigor and furnished information which was useful only to the opponents of the proposed cuts.

CEILING ON EXPENDITURES

A second type of congressional attempt to exert greater control over the defense appropriation was the Smith (Virginia) amendment to impose a ceiling on the actual amounts to be expended during the 1953 fiscal year. Giving loud and vocal claims to its prerogatives and the fear that purse control was slipping away, the House passed the ceiling amendment in an attempt to regain control over a huge backlog of unspent funds—about $57,000,000. The amendment was passed amidst warnings by Rep. John Vorys of

> a threat of a military dictatorship over the economy of our country by permitting the military to have the possibility of spending $103,000,000,000 in one year, if they so desire. This amendment will return to the Congress the responsibility they should carry out of deciding upon expenditures.[10]

Vorys was probably engaging in an oratorical flourish. The Defense Department could not possibly spend $103,000,000,000 in a year because of the long-range nature of Defense procurement. Nevertheless, the backlog of unspent appropriations can be used to cushion cuts in appropriations. Representative Frederic Coudert suggested prior Congresses "have frittered away to a very large extent the control over the power of the purse. . . . This amendment represents a first step, and a very important step, in reestablishing legislative power."[11]

Rising in support of the Smith amendment, the Republican Minority leader, Rep. Joseph W. Martin of Massachusetts, declared:

> A wall of secrecy has been developed in recent years between the Defense Department and other departments of our Government. We make appropriations, and after we have appropriated the money these bureaucrats no longer care about Congress. . . . We have almost abdicated the powers given us under the Constitution . . . we must recapture and regain control over the finances of our country.[12]

The limiting amendment was carried by a (division) vote of 168 to 77.

The House cuts and expenditure limitations brought sharp protests from the President and military chiefs, including threats of a special session of Congress to get the funds restored. Meanwhile, the Senate began its hearings on the bill, in which official rebuttal to some of the House arguments and actions was made. In its report the Senate Armed Services Appropriations Subcommittee eliminated the limit on expenditures but cut even further the overall amount. The Senate subcommittee report praised the House for its "laudable effort to reduce the cost of preparedness" but observed that the House's restricting amendment "would seriously impair the defense program by, in effect, rescinding appropriations and contract authorities approved by the Congress in the appropriation bills for prior years dating back as far as 1950." Apparently lecturing the House for its unwise action, the Senate report stated:

> Science and invention have increased the cost of war and of preparations for war and have made it costly in time as well as in dollars. Many of the implements of warfare which have been authorized by the Congress and for which contracts have been made, take from 12 to 36 months to construct.

How then was the Congress to control government spending? Said the report: "No effective limitation can be made upon current expenditures of this kind except by control of appropriations." The committee declared that this was what it was trying to do in recommending a figure $472,426,642 below the total House bill and over $5,500,000,000 below the President's requests. But it was unwilling to impose control on the basis of past appropriations and so eliminated the House-imposed ceiling.[13]

The Senate accepted its committee recommendation and omitted the expenditures ceiling. Probably under the pressure of military leaders and the Administration, the conferees also omitted the provision.

Had Congress imposed the ceiling amendment, there is no doubt but that it could have controlled the *amounts* to be expended by the Department of Defense. But it seems almost certain that it had no real idea of what the consequences of taking such action would have been because of the limitations of the information made available to it.

Conclusions

Perhaps the size and nature of the Defense appropriation is enough to demonstrate that Congress could not possibly have had sufficient information upon which to base its judgment and thus relied to a large extent on the meat-axe method of imposing cuts.

There can be little doubt that Congress and the subcommittee lacked the time, the competence, and the staff to do much more than snipe at the superficial aspects of the Defense appropriation bill. During the House debate, Rep. Richard Wigglesworth asserted bluntly that this bill, "the most important bill of the entire session . . . should not be here on this floor today." He stated that the bill had not had its deserved consideration. "We have not . . . been afforded proper opportunity for consideration of the facts which we should have at hand. We have not . . . been in a position to obtain facts which we should have at hand." He bitterly suggested that the bill would soon pass the House and then "slumber peacefully over in the Senate perhaps for the next three months."[14]

Even more outspoken on this question was Rep. Howard W. Smith of Virginia, who offered the amendment setting a limit on expenditures. He complained that the committee report had come to Members just as floor consideration began:

> I am just wondering, when we are presented with the final report on it this morning and expected to approve it in a day or two, how the gentleman's committee expects Members of the House to vote intelligently upon this enormous bill with as little information as we have, and when there is a very decided disagreement in the committee itself?

Mr. Taber admitted it was "going to be very difficult on a great many items in this bill to cast an intelligent vote." He observed that "two-thirds of those who sat in to mark up (the bill) had not been priviledged to attend hearings on items under consideration."[15]

Rep. Errett P. Scrivner of Kansas expressed similar thoughts from the standpoint of staff inadequacies, observing that

> there is no question but what the Appropriations Committee does not have an adequate staff of experts. If you could sit in our little committee rooms and see the heads of these technical services come in with their staffs, each one of them with 8, 9, 10, 11, 12, 15 all supporting him in his presentation, you see what we are up against.... Certainly we have to have more help.

For these and other reasons, Scrivner declared that, "We do not have the control that we should have.... I think the House of Representatives and the Committee on Appropriations loses almost entire control of earmarking funds for the military."[16] He was referring here in part to the transfer of funds by the Army to programs other than those designated in requests to Congress. Another protest against lack of access to adequate information came in this form from Rep. Thomas H. Werdel: "... we should have something besides the prepared manuscripts from the Pentagon in order to justify a favorable vote on this bill for this amount of money."[17]

Statements were made, it is true, that Congress did maintain its control, despite its shortcomings in securing adequate data. In opposing the House amendment to subject the Department of Defense to an expenditures ceiling, the Chairman of the House subcommittee, Rep. George Mahon of Texas stated, "Let me point out that Congress still keeps control of the purse strings, we can recover the money and we can cancel contracts that are outstanding by paying to industry a fair adjustment...." Further, "Since when have we lost control of the purse strings?" Passage of the bill as recommended by the committee, he declared, was the only "forthright and honest method of telling the American people what defense is costing them." But Mahon was whistling in the dark, or at least reaching for a debater's point to oppose the ceiling amendment. Shortly before, he had asserted that Members "have heard on all sides stories of waste and stupidity in the Defense Department...."[18] The majority leadership of the committee had concurred in the cut of roughly 10 percent, but were waging a floor fight against further cuts or expenditure limitation. Moreover, the

"Explanatory Notes" document prepared under Mahon's direction had stated:

> Justifications submitted in support of the budget requests were, in many respects, very unsatisfactory. The areas where the information was most unsatisfactory was due, in a large measure, to the failure of higher authority to make the necessary program decisions in time for proper and detailed consideration to be given to preparing supporting information. Particularly in the area of information concerning civilian personnel (commonly referred to as green-sheets) was the information inadequate. It was not possible from the information contained in the justifications to ascertain the number of personnel assigned or required to perform a certain project or function.[19]

Actually, the Appropriations Committees in Congress did not even approach possession of adequate data to exert control on the defense appropriation.

The Senate committee, which also opposed the expenditure limitation, was nevertheless cognizant of its lack of control and criticized the Defense Department for its recent practice of starting programs that were substantially larger than those provided for by appropriation bills passed by Congress. This, it was said, had the effect of "committing the Congress to these enlarged programs before they had been presented to the appropriate committees in detail or passed on by the House or Senate."[20]

Thus, Congress struggled with what one Senator described as "this titanic bill," and after resorting to various devices, indicating frustration relative to control of the purse and attempting various amendments, finally passed a bill that cut about 10 percent from the budget requests. The motive behind the cut, which was divided among the several defense services and functions, was to enforce economy and efficiency by means of the meat axe.

In the face of the huge amounts requested, there were definite indications of frustration in attempting to scrutinize defense requests and spending. There were pleas for more time, especially in the House, and for more adequate staffing. Congress exercised considerable power through amendments and through reducing the over-all amount on a meat-axe basis. Thus, while Congress has tremendous power over administration and policy through its appropriating process, it is highly doubtful that such power is *control* in view of Congress' oft-expressed frustrations about its inability to ascertain consequences.

Chapter 6

Cutting Down on Overhead

Congressional attacks on administrative overhead expenses, especially service activities, represent the third most common category of cuts. They are popular since, on the record at least, they permit Members to press for economy without seeming to hurt actual programs. All government activities represent service activities in a broad sense, but for our purposes we shall consider "service" in its direct context. The services provided by the General Services Administration, the Post Office, and the Veterans Administration are typical in this respect. All three agencies provide direct services but affect different groups of citizens.

VULNERABLE OVERHEAD

In its money requests for the 1953 fiscal year, the GSA's major appropriation item, "operating expenses," included the basic appropriation for its primary operation to act as "landlord" for other government agencies, and to establish and supervise systems of real property, personal property, and records management. The House committee recommended a sizeable reduction of 16½ percent to be spread out among the component parts of the operating expenses item, without giving any specific reasons for the vast bulk of the cut.[1] During the House floor debate, Rep. Albert Thomas of Texas, the chairman of the subcommittee in charge of the bill, stated that he had heard on street corners, in cloak rooms, and in conversations between Members generally, frequent mention of the overstaffing prevalent in government agencies. But in taking the side of the agencies, he said, "We, as Members of Congress year after year and day after day pass more laws, piling more duties and obligations upon the agencies of the Government, and as long as the Congress does that, they must increase their personnel."[2] Rep. John Phillips of California expressed his opinion that a thorough job had been done on the bill, without more adequate help. The Committee had reduced the bill by 16¼ percent, which he considered a good cut, upon those items controllable by Congress. He also said there was no way to cut expenditures without cutting some spot that is sensitive to someone.

Rep. Thomas Curtis of Missouri, however, stated that the "executive direction and staff operations" component of the operating expense item in the GSA estimates was a very difficult one to run down. He believed this to be top overhead, and therefore susceptible to reduction, and offered an amendment to cut the item by 25 percent. "As we can visualize it from the little information we have, it is mainly cutting the top overhead personnel, and should in no way effect the actual operation of the GSA in the field, where they are performing their functions."[3] Mr. Curtis' claim that the cut applied only to overhead and would not hurt the operating program was refuted by Mr. Thomas, who stated that 25 percent would be too crippling. Nevertheless, the amendment carried.

Meanwhile, Rep. William Dawson of Illinois offered an amendment for increasing the funds for building management, real property acquisition and utilization, and public-utilities management. He justified his amendment on the grounds that no allowance was being made the GSA for work being transferred to them. And Rep. M. G. Burnside of West Virginia offered an amendment which would have raised the funds allocated for the National Archives and Records Service. He cited as an example of the economies that this Service could produce, the operation at the records center at Alexandria, Virginia, where over a million dollars had been saved. Both the Dawson and the Burnside amendments were rejected, however.

The difficulties the GSA faces when it tries to secure adequate funds result primarily from the fact that it is an "overhead" agency whose operations do not directly affect large sections of the population. Overhead in expenditures is naturally a popular place to make reductions since those seeking cuts in this area assert that substantive program operations will not be harmed. It is not difficult to understand, therefore, why House floor amendments for reductions generally passed, despite the power of the committee, while amendments for increases, no matter how well justified, were summarily rejected.

Members of the committee and Congress generally took the GSA administrator's recommendations with a grain of salt. They had no means of disproving his points and relied on hunches about waste in overhead as a guide for their actions. Had independent analyses of GSA's operations been available, Congress might still have made the reductions, but they could have been made more realistically than the blind cuts that actually occurred. Had these independent analyses born out the testimony of Mr. Jess Larson, the GSA Administrator, then the GSA appropriation would probably have fared much better than it did, for these independent analyses can be used to protect agencies from cuts if they agree with the agencies' justification.

Impregnable Overhead

The elements of difficult evaluation involved in the GSA money requests applied also to the Post Office. Congress was forced to rely exclusively on the materials furnished by administrators, and large sums were for the purpose of overhead. But as a service operation with a great deal of overhead, the postal requests were accorded much more favorable treatment than those of the GSA for a very important reason: postal operations directly affect millions of people. The Post Office Department resembles other agencies of the federal government in that it depends upon Congress for appropriations to carry on its work. It differs from most other agencies in that its principal function is selling a service to the general public for which established charges are made. Thus it is essentially an earning agency, although its total expenses have exceeded its total revenues by large amounts in recent years. The Department actually spends the money it takes in from the public, drawing on the Federal Treasury only for funds in excess of revenues, but only within the limits of the total amounts specifically appropriated by Congress.[4]

House hearings for the Post Office Department appropriation are usually brief. In 1952, for example, they lasted only three days, covering a mere 163 pages of testimony.[5] At those hearings, the discussions centered mostly around reasons for requested increases in expenditures over the previous year. Postal authorities called attention to newly enacted pay increases for postal workers as well as adjustments in annual and sick leave for Department personnel, the increased cost of transportation, and an increase in the volume of mail to be handled. Moreover, the Postmaster General declared that many of the total operating costs of running the postal service were beyond the control of his Department. The vast bulk of postal expenses, he said, consisted of personnel and transportation costs. Personnel pay rates were established by Congress, while hauling rates were fixed by the Interstate Commerce Commission in the case of railroad transportation and by the Civil Aeronautics Board in the case of air transport.[6] This later prompted Congressman J. Vaughn Gray of Virginia to remark on the floor of the House that the Department controls only 3 percent of its expenditures, with the other 97 percent controlled by Congress, the ICC, and the CAB.[7]

The largest of the four Post Office appropriations items appearing in the bill under discussion was "postal operations." The estimate for the fiscal year 1953 for this item was $2,200,000,000, an increase of about $327,000,000 over funds voted for fiscal 1952. The increase was requested because of recently enacted salary increases, annual leave adjustments, and the anticipated increase in the volume of mail to be handled.[8] The House committee recommended a reduction of $27,000,000 under the estimate, a cut of only 1 percent. The committee report stated that it had taken into consideration the higher amounts made necessary because of salary increases and annual leave adjustments as well as the anticipated higher volume of mail.[9] It was not clear precisely how they intended the reduction to be applied.

Congressman Gary was the floor manager for the bill when it was presented in the House. In discussing it, he stated, "Frankly there is not very much that can be done about the Post Office Department appropriation,"[10] a remark indicative of the general feeling in Congress that control of postal appropriations was hopeless. In the case of postal operations, here was a single item which accounted for nearly one-fourth of all civilian operating expenditures of the entire Federal Government. Virtually all of Congress' information came from the Department concerned and no adequate means were available to cross-check any of it. Thus did the comments made on the floor center about such peripheral matters as the quality of service and the postal deficit, both of which were subjected to carping criticism without any real and positive suggestions for improvements. In the end, the House made no changes in its committee recommendations for the postal operations item.

The Senate hearings are also usually cursory, covering in 1952 only 152 pages of testimony in two days. The witnesses and testimony followed the same general pattern established in the earlier House hearings and the same tabular presentations were again used.[11] In its report for that year, the Senate committee recommended no change in the amount passed by the House.[12] On the floor of the Senate, Senator Homer Ferguson of Michigan offered a general amendment to reduce the total Post Office appropriation by $45,000,000. A second amendment offered by Senator Ferguson and Senator Styles Bridges of New Hampshire called for a reduction in amounts budgeted for travel expenses of 10 percent.[13] Still a third amendment was offered by Senator Everett Dirksen of Illinois which, he said, "would gear the expenditures to the appropriation, and would set a ceiling for it." Amidst demands for reductions in overhead, the Senate agreed to all three amendments, but all were deleted by the Conference Committee where it was noted that a reduction in the Post Office Department appropriation made several years previously had resulted in a curtailment of the postal delivery service which created a "flood of protests."[14] Thus, over two billion dollars became committed to the task of maintaining postal operations throughout the nation. The immensity of the size, scope and complexity of the Post Office Department prevented the appropriations items from being even to a small extent understood by Congress.

Who does control postal appropriations? The answer would appear to be: Nobody. On the one hand, Postmasters General delight in pointing out that, with pay rates, working conditions, and transportation rates, as well as postage rates and service charges, set by some other group, they do not control the amounts of money necessary to carry out the postal service. On the other hand, congressional committees held only five days of hearings on expenditures amounting, in all, to over two and three-quarter billion dollars—at a rate of over a half billion dollars a day, hardly adequate to even approach an understanding of the requirements. As a result, Congress will usually shy away from cutting funds for the Post Office because postal operations affect millions of citizens and there is no access to information other than that provided by postal officials. There is no real way of ascertaining the degree of efficiency or inefficiency with which the Post Office spends some three billion dollars of the taxpayers' money. Postal officials maintain that they must curtail services if Congress imposes large reductions and Members have no definite means of contradicting these assertions.

The field of postal appropriations is an area where Congress especially needs objective and capable analyses of expenditures if any degree of control over these expenditures is to be maintained. The Post Office Department is a mammoth, bulky operation, steeped in outmoded methods, overcentralized, and resistant to change. The Postmaster General's complaint that he had no control over postal costs was an evasion of his responsibility to Congress. Certainly pay rates are set by Congress and hauling rates by other agencies, but *numbers* of employees and how they are utilized and organized, the efficiency of hauling operations, and general organization and effectiveness can be affected by the Postmaster General. Yet Congress could not dare force any changes. Reduced appropriations could be met by curtailment of service with Congress taking the blame. Forced changes in organization and operation in the absence of definite knowledge of the consequences could also result in havoc.

Some of the flaws in postal operations have been obvious: horse and buggy rural routes in an automotive age; walking postmen on suburban routes where motorized tricycles could triple mail loads and length of routes; failure to use more mail sorting machines; woefully outmoded and inefficient equipment, including maintenance of overly expensive repair units; boundless red tape in a massive organization requiring Washington clearance on petty details. Congress must bear its share of the blame for these flaws, but independent analyses would help them to enact postal appropriations with more knowledge of the consequences of their actions than grudging reliance on the agency concerned.

In my judgement, the Post Office is an agency where overhead costs could more logically be attacked than would be the case of any other large department, and yet lack of information keeps it immune to sizable reductions. If Congress insists on reductions in overhead, and that would appear to be a valid approach if adequate information were to be available, then the Post Office should be the best place to initiate thorough expenditures analyses for uses in that direction.

HOMOGENIZATION OF OVERHEAD AND OPERATIONS

In discussing service items, we have reviewed appropriations items affecting the General Service Administration, whose operations directly affect very few people, and the Post Office Department, which directly affects the entire population. We turn now to a service which directly affects a sizeable portion of the population very intensely, the Veterans' Administration.

The GSA is politically impotent because of its lack of direct impact. The Post Office is not impotent, but its impact is so broad as to lose any concentration of political power. The VA represents still another color in the political spectrum. Its operations vitally affecting a huge number of citizens, it has clustered about its powerful veterans' organizations and is backed by an effective emotional appeal.

Thus a consideration of the VA in our efforts to survey the use of overhead reductions as a technique of Congress to control expenditures will help to round out our review of service operations in the appropriations process. Let us, therefore, consider the 1952 VA item, "administration, medical, hospital, and domiciliary services" (operating expenses). To compare the fate of this item with one of a more substantive nature, we should also consider "hospital and domiciliary facilities" (construction).

The administration item included all expenses of administration, salaries and operations of the Veterans' Administration in Washington and in field offices, the cost of travel and examination of beneficiaries, repairs and maintenance of equipment, payments to contract hospitals for the care of Veterans' Administration patients, supervision of veterans' education and training, and reimbursements for the care of eligible veterans in State soldiers' homes. The appropriation also covered the cost of such administration of veteran benefits as compensation and pensions, readjustment allowances, loans, insurance, and housing for certain classes of disabled veterans.[15] The 1953 budget request for administration was $895,000,000. The item for hospital and domiciliary facilities provided for the construction of new facilities, the acquisition of sites, alterations, major structural improvements, and equipment for Veterans' Administration hospital and domi-

PART II. *Techniques of Control*

ciliary facilities.[16] A review of the administration item, which is overhead, along with that for construction will enable us to assess the degree to which Congress attempted to economize on overhead while preserving the program itself.

During the 1952 House subcommittee hearing, a lively controversy arose over the availability of and demand for VA hospital beds. The VA planned to add 15,000 new hospital and domiciliary beds to its program during 1953. Rep. Thomas quoted newspaper talk to the effect that the VA had more beds available than patients to fill them. He also commented on the VA's figures, which indicated an apparent 20 percent bed vacancy rate, and that with additional beds still planned, the vacancy percentage would rise to 25 or 30 percent. He then called attention to assertions that either the vote-conscious Congress overdid it or that the VA could not get patients for its hospitals. General Carl Gray, VA Administrator, admitted that there were certain hospitals the VA was unable to fill and regarded the cause as due partly to an insufficient time-lapse for the patient-load to arrive. In reply to Mr. Thomas' query whether it was time to halt further hospital construction, he made no strong case for the item, simply stating that it was in the discretion of Congress, which had ordered the hospitals built in the first place.[17]

The House committee recommended reductions in the administration of the VA hospital program by cutting the "nonmedical" phases of what they apparently considered overhead costs. These reductions amounted to $91,400,000 from the total request of $895,000,000.[18] No reductions were made, however, in the $153,000,000 request for construction of "hospital and domiciliary facilities." One can only conclude, since substantial reductions were made only in the "nonmedical" (overhead) phases of the veterans hospital program, that the House committee looked at cuts in actual hospital construction with some trepidation, fearing the wrath of the veterans' groups.

During the Senate subcommittee hearings, General Gray sought to restore the House cut. He declared that unless this were done, the VA would have to eliminate many urgent projects from its 1953 program and would further delay a long-needed program for modernization of buildings. The House cut presented an unsolvable problem, according to Gray, since it required drastic curtailment of the quantity of services and medical care that was available for eligible veterans. Not only, he said, did the House action completely disregard staffing requirements for new hospitals included in the program approved by the President and Congress, but it required a reduction of 2,473 from the present staff in existing hospitals and homes.[19] Apparently impressed with General Gray's testimony, the Senate subcommittee recommended that the administration item be increased by $68,000,000 over the House figure, but that the hospital construction item be reduced from $153,000,000 to $66,000,000.[20] Gray had made no strong plea for hospital construction, directing his remarks instead to restoration of the House cuts in the administration item. The full Senate accepted its committee recommendations without controversy. The Conference Committee arrived at its final figure by splitting the difference between the House and Senate figures evenly.

The general sources of information made available to Members of Congress concerning the VA appropriation included VA representatives, newspaper editorials and articles, and varied statistical compilations dealing with numerous phases of the VA program compiled largely by the VA, the American Legion, and other veterans' organizations. Congress also received communications from such correspondents as university medical faculty members, legislative liaison bureaus of organizations like the American Legion, Disabled American Veterans, and the Veterans of Foreign Wars, State legislators, and private individuals, including veterans and doctors. Hearsay evidence, such as cloakroom and sidewalk conversations, must also be considered a source. Many letters had been introduced in the Senate hearings representing the views of veterans' organization officers, medical practitioners, and private individuals. The high percentage of vetterans, veterans' organizations, and other groups responding indicates that a considerable exchange of information and exhortation must have taken place under the guidance of or at the direction of the various professional veteran groups. One identical communication, for example, had been received from thirty-six separate individuals. A disproportionate amount of time was devoted to debate on the House floor concerning the contact services provided by the VA. Less than 1 percent of the funds provided in the administration item was involved. Yet many more millions of dollars were underlying other and much broader aspects of the VA's budget requests, where little or no debate was involved.

The American Legion and other veterans' organizations maintain alert and competent professional staffs which critically examine those actions of Congress which concern veterans and the VA. These staffs also regularly prepare detailed analytical statements for the press, Members of Congress, and other interested groups. The primary objective is to further the interests of the individual veteran, but concomitantly those of the VA are also frequently abetted.

Congress treats VA money requests with a vastly greater degree of thoroughness than the GSA and Post Office appropriations. VA programs vitally affect millions of voters and require more attention from politically conscious Congressmen than mere overhead and housekeeping operations such as those carried out by the General Services Administration, or a broad general service such as that of the Post Office. But it is also a fact that the VA administration item was nearly ten times the size of the GSA's operating expenses.

On the VA requests themselves, we note that the House attempted to economize on overhead by reducing the administration item but left untouched the request for construction of hospitals despite the demonstrated lack of need. The House went overboard in its attempt to reduce overhead without hurting the program. The Senate, however, recognized that drastic cuts in overhead must adversely affect the VA's program and restored much of the House reduction on the administration item. Moreover, it recognized the lack of need for hospitals and cut back the construction request, even though the request represented substantive phases of the VA program.

In the consideration of a VA request such as that for administration, amounting to nearly a billion dollars, there would appear to be an even greater need for independent expenditure analyses. The item is politically and emotionally charged, with information coming primarily from the VA and veterans' groups. Independent analyses would seem to offer an offsetting and objective set of data for Congress to consider as well as that presented by agencies and groups involved in the program.

Chapter 7

The "Pork Barrel"

Projects and Politics

Congressional attempts to control federal spending are not limited to economy efforts. Instead they may very well be aimed at raising the ante for favorite programs, a situation which often pits Member against Member as well as Congress against the Executive. This occurs most frequently in the case of federal construction projects beneficial to certain regions.

Localities and private concerns which profit from projects constructed at the expense of the general taxpayers have come to accept the Federal Treasury as fair game, and the congressional lawmaking and appropriating powers cause these groups to press their demands through Congress. Their power, wielded by publicity, votes, and campaign contributions, causes Congressmen to listen attentively to their requests. Even if a lawmaker has no desire to curry their favor by securing enactment of their programs, he will still try to avoid incurring their enmity. Of course, all construction projects cannot be categorized as purely of a local nature. Some waterways, for example, are important arteries of interstate commerce and bring about a greater volume of cheap, water-borne transportation. Others provide a needed growth in the availability of electric power for defense industries. Still others make the greatest use of natural power sites and provide integrated development of river valleys, which states or private enterprise cannot do.[1]

Most of the appropriations items for civilian construction are included in two measures. The Civil Functions Appropriation Bill contains funds for rivers, harbors and flood control programs administered by the U. S. Army Corps of Engineers, and the Department of the Interior appropriation bill provides money for multipurpose water projects constructed by the Bureau of Reclamation. Chambers of commerce or other local improvement groups initiate practically all Corps of Engineers civilian construction projects. These groups solicit support of their local Congressman and their Senators, who are anxious to please their constituents. In fact, they frequently feel that the price of political survival is to do so. Members of Congress, therefore, go to Washington determined to get the necessary appropriation, but they soon discover that virtually every one of the 535 Members of the two Houses of Congress has a similar mission. The only way a Congressman can get his own project included in the final bill is to make an open or tacit agreement that he will support similar, if less meritorious, projects advanced by his colleagues. A completed bill is built up by this process of mutual accommodation. The result is a bill which, as one of its sponsors remarked, "has something in it for everybody."[2] Irrigation and power projects of the Department of the Interior have a similar development although they are more likely to originate from general surveys conducted by the Bureau of Reclamation.

Agency operations are not geographically restricted but, generally, the Corps of Engineers constructs most of its projects in the eastern and southern portions of the country, the Bureau of Reclamation concentrates in the southwest and west, while both administer programs in the midwest. Obviously, then, a congressional coalition of construction advocates would represent a formidable force in Congress. Having experienced efforts to reduce funds for these projects, Senator Paul Douglas has been led to write:

> The student of legislation is forced to wonder upon occasion if there is not some informal understanding between the advocates of irrigation projects and the supporters of the rivers and harbors projects. Each group seems to support the other or at least does not disturb the serenity of the other's dovecots.[3]

The Army Engineers and Bureau of Reclamation gather voluminous data to justify their expenditures. Once a project has received legislative authorization, the agencies will gladly develop such information. Huge difficulties face the Member who seeks to reduce such expenditures, however, for he faces opposition not only from the agencies, but from other Members of Congress as well.

Moreover, unless the individual Member desires early retirement, he will weigh the political consequences of his actions. If he seeks economy, he must maintain consistency and accept cuts on projects dear to the hearts of his own constituents as well as those of other Members. He may attempt to solve this problem, as did Senator Douglas during the early 1950's, by appealing to the general interest even within his own district. Politically, this is a calculated risk. Douglas felt that the fault of excessive "pork barrel" expenditures rested primarily with the localities which turned the "heat" on their Congressmen. But he has also felt that Congressmen erred in picturing their constituents as narrow-minded and greedy, and that they ought to explain the national needs to their constiuents as well as to work for their local interests. On one occasion, on the floor of the Senate, he stated:

> I know only too well what we are up against. Local groups demand that their Representative and Senators bring home the "bacon" or else. All too often these groups loudly proclaim their desire for economy, but at the same time they want their local pet projects at the Federal Government's expense. They want economy practiced on the other fellow, but not on themselves. . . . Yet I sometimes feel that we underestimate the amount of citizen statesmanship which is actually in existence. Too often we picture our constituents as selfish, greedy individuals constantly demanding more and more for themselves. . . . But . . . I have found local leaders very understanding and with a sincere desire to put the national interest first.[4]

It is somewhat doubtful whether a Member of Congress from a district greatly benefiting from federal appropriations could make the same plea without losing his political life. Senator Douglas was re-elected in 1954, but so many other factors entered into the Illinois political picture that the political success or failure of appealing to the general interest will probably remain untested. As we have stated, it is a calculated risk.

DAMS AND DIKES

The Corps of Engineers develop specific economic justification for their rivers and harbors and flood control projects. Commenting on the planning reports furnished by the Corps, the House subcommittee report on the Civil Functions' appropriation for 1953 stated:

> The inability of the Corps of Engineers to furnish the committee with firm obligation and expenditure data is becoming increasingly apparent and can only be attributable to inadequate management and

budgetary practices. The responsibility for this unwarranted condition rests largely not only with the Corps of Engineers but with the Bureau of the Budget. This latter agency has failed in this instance to present to the Congress accurate and adequate information. This can only point to the lack of proper screening of the data submitted in justification of budget requests of the Corps of Engineers.[5]

Although the subcommittee indicated that submission of requested information in future reports should result in the Corps presenting to the Congress sound and complete information on their civil works program, the above quotation is indicative of the subcommittee's complete reliance on the Corps for information. Yet these programs are sizable. The budget request for Army civil functions for fiscal 1953 contained over a half billion dollars in funds for seventy-six flood control construction proposals and twenty-six river and harbor projects.[6] Unlike items for salaries and expenses or operations of an agency with a continuing service to perform, construction estimates are justified principally on a project cost basis. Since many projects are started or completed each year, the annual project allocation does not necessarily bear a direct relationship to the previous year's appropriations allocation. For example, the rivers and harbors appropriation for 1953 was 23 percent *over* while the flood control appropriation was 29 percent *under* the figure for the previous year.

The largest single item in the Department of the Interior appropriation bill is for construction and rehabilitation in the Bureau of Reclamation. As the name implies, it provides funds for construction and rehabilitation of reclamation and multiple-purpose water projects in the seventeen western States. Special acts of Congress authorizing specific reclamation projects frequently go into considerable detail, spelling out repayment plans, citing features that can be constructed, and establishing authorization for nonreimbursable allocations. Committee hearings on these projects tend to be loaded down with justification. House committee hearings on the Interior appropriation for 1953, for example, appeared in four volumes, of which about 900 pages related to the Bureau of Reclamation, and primarily the item for construction and rehabilitation.[7] The hearings included various statements offered by departmental officials in justification of the estimates, and testimony offered by Members of Congress, interested organizations, and individuals. Aside from a few witnesses appearing before the committee in opposition to certain power transmission lines, some twenty Members of Congress and over a hundred individuals and representatives of organizations spoke in support of projects in their respective States.

Senate subcommittee hearings consisted of 1,620 pages, half of which pertained to the Bureau of Reclamation item for construction and rehabilitation.[8] The basic material presented was much the same as that given before the House subcommittee with emphasis on restoration of the reductions which had been made by the House. In addition to Department witnesses, seventeen Members of Congress, mostly Senators and all from the seventeen Reclamation States, appeared before the subcommittee in favor of restoration of funds for specific projects or the restoration of planning funds within their respective States.

Conclusions

In studying the appropriations process on construction items, one notes the tendency for the House to make drastic reductions in the budget requests, the Senate to restore most of these cuts, and the conference committee to split the differences between the two figures. We have already seen in Chapter II that among the reasons for House stringency and Senate generosity among the civil functions and interior appropriations subcommittees is the way the membership is determined. House subcommittee members, selected by the full committee chairman, tend to represent areas which have no "stake" in the construction items. Senate subcommittee members, chosen on the basis of personal choice backed up by seniority tend to represent States with large "stakes" in these bills.

On all major construction items, there is normally heavy reliance on the House and Senate Appropriations Subcommittees' action by the full Appropriations Committees and by the House and the Senate. In 1952, all efforts to raise or lower by either specific or percentage methods were rejected. The reliance of Congress upon the judgment of these subcommittees emphasizes the power of these small groups and calls for a consideration of what they relied on for their judgments. In the case of rivers and harbors and flood control, it was almost exclusively the Corps of Engineers, which was the construction agency that wanted the money to spend, individual Congressmen, and individuals and representatives of organizations from all over the United States pleading for funds for projects for their respective areas. The Corps spoke convincingly in defense of the President's budget, and, on request, readily gave figures to show the budget action on their original submissions. The justifications appeared to be, however, generally in the narrow framework of relating the benefits accuring from an authorized project to a particular region or locality. Generally lacking was any testimony in the interest of economy, directly relating the need for appropriations for public works to the defense needs of the nation or to reduction of the deficit.

The information as to need, relative priority, and the cost of reclamation projects also comes from the executive agencies and from interested parties, which included in this case thirty-seven statements from western Senators and Representatives.

Types of information which were not apparently available to the Congress and which would have assisted them in their action were as follows:

1. Direct statements from Department of Defense or other executive officials as to the defense values, if any, of the construction program.
2. Reasons for the actions of the Bureau of the Budget in modifying the original estimates of the Corps of Engineers and Bureau of Reclamation.
3. Information from the field or regions as to the relative priority or need of a new project or item in relationship to other regional or local needs requiring federal funds under a limited budget.
4. More precise information as to the national, regional or local benefits to be derived from the construction of any project. The basic and authorizing legislation may require very little local participation in costs and not take sufficiently into consideration the local benefits. This would leave the Appropriations Committees little control over this factor, and, at the same time, cause hundreds of protagonists to appear in support of projects wholly or primarily financed through federal funds. These "interests" would probably have been much less aggressive, were there a larger contribution required from the local people or the users of the proposed facility.

The provisions approved by the Congress in 1952 raise serious questions as to final inclusion of individual projects, particularly the new starts. The selection of projects appeared to be haphazard, with committee members mentioning such things as allowing the same figure as in the previous years, vast sums going into foreign

Sciences de la gestion
UNIVERSITÉ
OTTAWA
UNIVERSITY
Management Sciences

aid, the backlog of authorized projects, and, in general terms, the increased wealth added by their construction, all to justify the relatively large appropriation from an economy-minded Congress.

One of the most significant shortcomings in congressional action on these projects was its failure to set up standards or criteria for selecting a hard core of high priority for defense-related projects. The reluctance on the part of the Corps of Engineers and the Bureau of Reclamation to provide relative priorities between projects or portions of projects was an obvious deficiency. Both played up the more or less equal popular appeal of all projects in the estimates.

With the knowledge that there is no congressional staff for broad impartial analysis of public works projects, and the recognition of the terrific pressures, one way of supplying the information lacked by the committees would appear to be an objective audit or analysis of the spending agencies' requests by a staff of engineer analysts reporting to the Congress. Such a group not only could be qualified to seek out the facts but might relate its activities to those of the authorization committees and other committees of Congress with a view to working out a realistic long-range program for rivers and harbors, flood control, and reclamation, geared, to the extent possible, into the peaks and troughs of the national economy.

The most fruitful advance in the consideration of funds for construction projects would be the development of standards and priorities which would take into account the degree of economic justification, national significance, and even local needs. In addition, localities and groups which benefit should share in the costs to the extent that the construction of a project would be considered as a joint enterprise rather than a political plum. The establishment of standards and priorities would permit Congress to appropriate money in any amounts with the assurance that the highest priority projects would go forward first. This would not prevent Congress from making exceptions, but the weight of the evidence before Congress as a whole would rest with the established standards.

Chapter 8

Painting Pretty Pictures— Politics and Procedures

As discussed in Chapter 2, authority for the agencies to spend money may take any one of a variety of forms. The final tallies as to the amounts appropriated and the cuts in the budget estimates include only one of these forms, however; namely, direct authorization to spend. Reappropriations, which reauthorize the spending of money previously appropriated, but which the agencies have not spent by the end of the fiscal year, do not show up in the final count. When Congress "reappropriates" instead of "appropriating," we have one of several methods of "painting pretty pictures" of economy without any substance of savings whatsoever. The purpose of this chapter is to discuss, with special emphasis on budgetary legerdemain, the total actions on a budget in transition— a budget prepared by one political administration but presented by another, and then reviewed by a Congress controlled by the same political party as the new administration.

Acute political controversy has historically surrounded the level of government expenditures, and recent years have been no exception. Big government, as we know it today, grew up under the exigencies of depression, war, and cold war which paralleled a national administration controlled by the Democratic Party. The twenty-year period 1932–52 witnessed marked increases in the level of federal expenditures under the leadership of the Democrats, a fact which Republicans seized upon as political issue from the beginning of the Democratic era. The presidential campaign year 1952 saw no letup in the use of this issue. Thus, when the Republicans came to power in January, 1953, controlling both Congress and the Executive, it was to be expected and even demanded, that the fiscal policies of the previous Democratic administrations be drastically altered.

That federal expenditures should be a campaign issue is especially important to us because it concerns congressional control of appropriations. Since in 1952 the Republicans won the Presidency and took over the leadership of both Houses of Congress, we need to analyze the impact of this change in relation to our inquiry. What did the new administration do about the problem of congressional control of expenditures? Were changes or improvements made? Did the new administration employ new methods in the executive branch making any changes in congressional procedures unnecessary? Did Congress, under new leadership, make any alterations to help the legislative branch consider expenditure requests? To answer these questions, we need to survey both executive and congressional action on the 1953–54 budget.

PLAYING WITH FIGURES

Let us initiate the inquiry with the asserted final results. At the close of the First Session of the 83d Congress, Senator Styles Bridges of New Hampshire, Chairman of the Senate Appropriations Committee, issued a statement summarizing the actions of that Congress on appropriations.[1] This document was used extensively by Republican orators in the 1954 political campaigns. Republican Members of Congress cited the figures in newsletters to constituents. Republican National Committee Chairman Leonard Hall also employed the figures and, reaching the broadest audience of all, President Eisenhower used them in a widely heralded radio-television Report to the Nation.[2] In fact, the results cited by Senator Bridges formed the groundwork of one of the new administration's major "accomplishments"—the elimination of wasteful spending.

Because of its widespread use, the Bridges statement needs careful examination. Its tone and purpose were set forth clearly in stating that:

> a major fiscal change [has taken] place.... The Congress ... and the President ... reversed a 20-year trend in Government spending and took steps which, in the years to come, will enable the Government to balance the budget and return the country to a sound fiscal policy.[3]

The statement asserted that President Eisenhower had cut former President Truman's budget requests by $9,500,000,000 and that

SAMPLE POLITICAL ADVERTISEMENT CITING
BUDGETARY SAVINGS OF EISENHOWER
ADMINISTRATION, 1954

Belleville, Ill. News-Democrat Mon 1 Nov 54

POLITICAL ADVERTISEMENT   POLITICAL ADVERTISEMENT   POLITICAL ADVERTISEMENT

GO AHEAD ... BLAME ME,
I VOTED REPUBLICAN

Blame me for stopping American bloodshed on the bleak and barren hills of Korea

Blame me for the 14 billion dollar reduction in the federal budget

Blame me for 10% reduction in taxes

Blame me for the return of honor and honesty in government

Blame me for replacing blood economy with sound economy

Blame me for protecting our American way of life from Socialistic trends

Blame me for reducing the cost of government

Blame me for prosperity with peace

Blame me for broadening Social Security

Blame me for replacing government controls with free enterprise

AND I'LL VOTE STRAIGHT REPUBLICAN AGAIN ... WOULDN'T YOU?

(This ad paid for by the Republican candidates who seek election)

PAINTING PRETTY PICTURES

Congress had made further reductions of $4,600,000,000. Arithmetic was then employed to demonstrate that total reductions made by the Republicans in the Truman budgetary requests were $14,100,000,000—on the face of it, a most impressive record documenting the claims of economies achieved by the Republicans. Many of the orators stopped here—"We cut the Truman budget requests by $14,000,000,000." This reduction was used as a major campaign issue in 1954, especially in paid political advertisements which appeared in the press. The reaction to these statements naturally varied according to the degree of sophistication of those addressed. At one level, it meant that the Republicans had cut annual federal expenditures by the stated amounts—that is, among those who did not realize the difference between appropriations and expenditures. At a slightly higher level of sophistication it meant that the new administration had trimmed Truman requests for appropriations for the fiscal year 1953–54 by $14,000,000,000. As we shall see, one would have had to possess an even higher degree of sophistication to realize that no such cuts had actually been made.

The Bridges statement continued with praise of the administration and the appropriations committees. "The success of our examination is proved in the further reductions made by Congress," it said.[4]

REVISING THE ESTIMATES

Acting on the 1953–54 Truman budget was in two parts: review by the administration and formulation of revised estimates, and congressional review. Let us first analyze the administrative action on the 1954 Truman budget and follow this with a review of congressional action.

Naturally, because it was most pressing, the first order of business for the new administration was to rework the Truman budget requests so that Congress could go about its business of appropriating funds to continue the federal government's operations. Senator Bridges has told how

> the chairman of the Senate Appropriations Committee conferred with the chairman of the House Appropriations Committee, with the new Director of the Bureau of the Budget, and with President Eisenhower.... It was decided at these meetings against formulating an entirely new budget document in the time available, but rather that

the departments should submit individual revisions of these original budget estimates as soon as practicable.[5]

The new Budget Director, Joseph M. Dodge, issued a call to all agencies directing a review of all appropriations requests with an eye to reduction. These, as quickly as they became available and cleared through the Budget Bureau, were presented to the press and to the congressional Appropriations Committees. The latter, meanwhile, conducted hearings and gathered information as far as possible until the revised estimates were sent through.

Considering the goals and the pressure of time, the new administration did a rather remarkable job in reviewing and reducing the Truman money requests for the fiscal year 1954. Paring down such requests by more than $9,000,000,000 with no more elimination of service than that asserted seems impressive indeed. How did they do it? The first point to catch the eye of the appropriations analyst is the similarity of the reductions to those voted by the Democratic 82d Congress, Second Session, in 1952. The latter cut Truman's 1953 money requests by $8,400,000,000 billion while President Eisenhower reduced Truman's 1954 requests by $9,300,000,000. Thus there was less than a billion dollars difference between the reductions voted by Congress in 1952 on the Truman budget for the fiscal year 1953 and those proposed by the new administration in early 1953 on the Truman budget for the fiscal year 1954.

The closeness of the total reductions proposed by Eisenhower and those voted by Congress for the previous year warrants closer scrutiny. A comparison of the two sets of cuts appears in Table 6. Reviewing the comparison of the appropriations bills in this table, we see that, in the cases of the Treasury and Post Office, Independent Offices, and Interior bills, the Eisenhower reductions below the Truman requests were greater than those applied by the 82d Congress to Truman's previous budget. But note that these reductions were accomplished by holding the new requests to about the same level as the appropriations enacted by Congress for fiscal 1953. On the Mutual Security requests, the Eisenhower cuts were greater than those of the 82d Congress, but reductions shown for Congress, to use comparable figures, would have been $1,500,-000,000, instead of $500,000,000, if reductions shown were the amounts below the original request, as is the case with the Eisenhower reduction.

Table 6

COMPARISON OF REDUCTIONS IN TRUMAN BUDGET REQUESTS: CONGRESSIONAL REDUCTIONS OF 1953 REQUESTS, AND EISENHOWER REDUCTIONS IN 1954 REQUESTS, REGULAR APPROPRIATIONS BILLS

(Millions of Dollars)

Bill	1953 Truman Requests	Amount of 1953 Requests Passed by Congress	Reductions by Congress in 1953 Truman Requests	1954 Truman Requests	1954 Eisenhower Requests	Reductions by Eisenhower in 1953 Truman Requests
Departments of Treasury and Post Office	3,515	3,438	77	3,572	3,449	123
The Independent Offices bills (one bill for 1953, two for 1954)	6,982	6,273	710	7,628	6,501	1,127
Department of Labor and Federal Security Agency (FSA became the Department of Health, Education and Welfare in 1953)	1,984	1,787	196	2,098	2,022	77
Department of Interior	632	542	90	607	491	116
Departments of State, Justice, Commerce	1,243 [a]	1,016 [a]	227 [a]	1,469	1,272	197
Legislative	86	77	9	114 [a]	114 [a]	0 [a]
Civil Functions, Department of the Army	713	584	129	683	499	185
Department of Agriculture	932	838	94	750	704	46
Department of Defense	51,391	46,611	4,780	40,720	35,772	4,948
Mutual Security Agency	6,493 [b]	6,002 [b]	484 [b]	7,614	5,139	2,475
Supplemental	13,868 [b]	11,794 [b]	2,074 [b]	1,035	1,071	37
Total	80,726	72,971	8,387	66,303	57,045	9,258

[a] Includes funds for the Judiciary.

[b] The 1953 Supplemental bill included Mutual Security. The 1953 reduction for Mutual Security is understated. The reduction shown is that made below the final appropriations request rather than the original budget estimate. The comparable reduction would be $1,500,000,000 below the original estimate of $7,900,000,000.

[c] Figures rounded and do not add up to totals.

Source: Bridges, *Record on Appropriations*, pp. 6–7; and Cong. Rec. (Daily Ed.), July 22, 1952, p. D718.

The Eisenhower reductions in the Truman 1954 estimates were greater than those applied by Congress to Truman's 1953 figures in the case of the Civil Functions and Defense appropriations, but congressional cuts were larger than those of Eisenhower on the State, Justice, Commerce, Agriculture, and Labor-Department of Health, Education and Welfare bills.

Thus we begin to develop an hypothesis with respect to how the new administration formulated its revised budgetary requests. By and large, it reviewed congressional action on Truman's previous budget, made comparable reductions, and then submitted them in the form of revised requests. We know at the outset that this was not invariably true (for example, reductions proposed for future commitments under the Agricultural Conservation Payment Program and Air Force cuts). Nevertheless, a general item-by-item review of all the appropriation requests, indicates this pattern, as is shown in Table 7.

Table 7 shows that over 90 percent of the 363 revised items surveyed were virtually the same, higher, or only slightly lower than either the Truman requests or the 1953 appropriation. Only 34 out of the 363 revised items represented great reductions below the 1953 appropriations and the 1954 Truman request. (To be a "great" reduction, for our purposes, the revised request had to be over $200,000 below both the 1954 Truman request and the 1953 appropriation, and over 10 percent below both of these amounts.)

Of further interest is an analysis of the 34 items substantially reduced. Table 8 lists all these items and indicates whether the cut was real or merely a paper saving. An "unreal" or "paper" saving is a reduction which will not, in any way, lower expenditures. For example, cutting an appropriation for meeting actual government commitments previously made in accordance with statutory authority represents no saving since, ultimately, the appropriation must be enacted. Table 8 shows that 8 of the 34 great reductions, nearly one-fourth of the total, were reductions for which credit cannot be claimed. The total of these unreal cuts below the Truman budget requests amounted to $440,000,000. When this amount is subtracted from the $900,000,000 by which the Eisenhower cuts exceeded the 1952 congressional cuts, the difference is less than a half billion dollars.

Thus far, we can see that reductions made by the revised estimates on civilian items were quite similar to those made by the

Table 7

SIGNIFICANCE OF EISENHOWER REDUCTIONS IN ITEMS INCLUDED IN THE 1954 TRUMAN BUDGET REQUESTS

Agency or Program	Number of Major Items	Number of Reductions Below Truman Budget	Items Where Proposals Were Virtually the Same Figures as the 1954 Truman Requests or Those Enacted for 1953 (Slightly less, the same, or Slightly Greater)	Items Which Represent a Great Reduction*
Department of agriculture...	53	42	49	1
Civil Functions.............	11	10	8	2
Independent Offices.........	75	5	70	8
Department of Commerce...	41	33	36	5
Department of Interior......	52	38	45	7
Department of Justice.......	13	9	13	0
Department of Labor.......	14	13	14	0
Department of Health, Education and Welfare........	68	44	63	6
Post Office.................	4	3	3	1
Department of State........	15	11	13	2
Department of Treasury.....	17	15	15	2
Total...............	363	223	329	34

*A "great" reduction, for our purposes, is one where the revised request was over $200,000 below both the 1954 Truman request and the 1953 appropriation and over 10 percent below both of these amounts.

The following are not included: Legislative bill (Executive does not tamper with this). District of Columbia bill (appropriations mostly repaid by local taxation). Defense bill (inclusion of Korean War costs in Eisenhower budget makes comparison impossible). Mutual Security bill (passed in separate bills; different item arrangement).

Source: Senate Committee on Appropriations, *Appropriation Acts and Reports* (Committee Print), 83d Cong., 1st Sess. (1953), and *Comparison of Original Estimates and Revised Estimates, 1954, by Departments, in Regular Bills* (Committee Print), 83d Cong., 2d Sess. (1954).

Table 8

ANALYSIS OF 34 APPROPRIATIONS ITEMS IN TRUMAN 1954 REQUESTS SUBSTANTIALLY REDUCED IN REVISED REQUESTS

Appropriation Bill and Item	1953 Appropriation (Millions)	1954 Truman Requests (Millions)	1954 Revised Request (Millions)	Reduction Below Truman Request (Millions)	Reduction Below 1953 Appropriation (Millions)	Real or Unreal Reduction
Department of Agriculture:						
1. Conservation and use of agricultural land resources, Production and Marketing Administration.	$251.7	$252.4	$212.0	$40.4	$ 39.7	Unreal[1]
Civil Functions:						
1. Construction, Rivers and Harbors and Flood Control.	404.8	491.3	332.3	159.0	72.5	Real
2. Flood Control, Mississippi River and Tributaries.	59.4	62.7	52.5	10.2	6.9	Real
Independent Offices:						
1. Atomic Energy Commission, Plant and Equipment.	3,270.5	436.4	166.0	270.4	3,104.5	Real
2. Strategic and Critical Materials.	134.0	188.0	0	188.0	134.0	Unreal[2]
3. Strategic and Critical Materials, Liquidation of Contracts	70.0	37.0	0	37.0	70.0	Unreal[2]
4. National Advisory Committee for Aeronautucis, Construction and Equipment	16.7	14.6	7.2	7.4	9.5	Real
5. Selective Service System.	36.8	34.4	29.9	4.5	6.9	Real

Item						
6. Tennessee Valley Authority.	336.0	254.0	190.8	63.6	145.2	Real
7. Veterans Administration, Hospital and Domiciliary Facilities	49.8	92.4	0	92.4	49.8	Unreal[3]
8. Veterans Administration, Major Alterations, Improvements, etc.	8.8	7.3	0	7.3	8.8	Real
Department of Commerce:						
1. Civil Aeronautics Administration, Establishment of Air Navagation Facilities.	9.9	13.0	7.0	6.0	2.9	Real
2. Civil Aeronautics Administration, Liquidation of Contract Authority.	3.6	7.0	0	7.0	3.6	Unreal[4]
3. Federal Airport Program.	14.3	30.0	0	30.0	14.3	Real
4. Bureau of Public Roads, Forest Highways.	18.0	20.0	15.0	5.0	3.0	Real
5. Bureau of Public Roads, Access Roads.	28.0	20.0	15.0	5.0	13.0	Real
Department of Interior:						
1. Office of the Secretary, Construction, Southeastern Power Administration.	0.7	6.7	0.1	6.6	0.6	Real
2. Office of the Secretary, Southwest Power Administration, Construction.	4.2	1.5	0	1.5	4.2	Real
3. Bonneville Power Administration, Construction.	66.5	55.2	47.2	8.0	19.3	Real
4. Bureau of Reclamation, Construction and Rehabilitation.	177.8	193.9	145.0	48.9	32.8	Real
5. Bureau of Mines, Construction.	3.6	1.8	0.4	1.4	3.2	Real
6. Office of Territories, Alaska Public Works.	13.2	15.0	10.0	5.0	3.2	Real
7. Office of Territories, Construction of Roads, Alaska.	17.0	18.4	14.6	3.8	2.4	Real

Table 8 (Continued)

Appropriation Bill and Item	1953 Appropriation (Millions)	1954 Truman Requests (Millions)	1954 Revised Request (Millions)	Reduction Below Truman Request (Millions)	Reduction Below 1953 Appropriation (Millions)	Real or Unreal Reduction
Department of Health, Education & Welfare:						
1. Howard University, Construction of Buildings (Liquidation of Contract Authority).	1.1	1.9	0	1.9	1.1	Real[5]
2. Office of Education, Promotion of Vocational Education.	18.6	18.7	14.0	4.7	4.6	Real
3. Public Health Service, Control of Venereal Diseases.	9.8	8.3	6.7	1.6	3.1	Real[6]
4. Public Health Service, Control of Tuberculosis.	8.2	7.6	5.7	1.9	2.5	Real
5. Public Health Service, Grants for Hospital Construction.	75.0	75.0	60.0	15.0	15.0	Real
6. Public Health Service, Construction of Research Facilities (Liquidation of Contract Authority).	3.2	3.0	2.5	0.5	0.7	Unreal[7]
Post Office Department:						
1. Transportation of Mails.	616.0	634.8	574.7	60.1	41.3	Unreal[8]
Department of State:						
1. Acquisition of Buildings, Abroad.	6.5	15.0	5.0	10.0	1.5	Unreal[9]
2. International Boundary & Water Commission, U.S. & Mexico, Construction.	13.7	9.3	6.6	2.7	7.1	Real
Department of the Treasury:						
1. Coast Guard, Acquistion, Construction, etc.	24.3	25.0	2.5	22.5	21.8	Real

PART II. *Techniques of Control*

[1] The commitments of funds for this program are made by the government in advance of appropriation. If the amount appropriated is insufficient to meet these commitments, the deficiency must be ultimately appropriated. Both House and Senate Committee Reports made it clear that the reduction was not to be construed as being a cutback in the program itself.

[2] These two reductions were unreal because they were made possible by a change in the estimates of funds already available. As of February 28, 1953, there was an unobligated balance of $457.7 million in the fund, available until expended, making additional appropriations unnecessary.

[3] This reduction represented no positive cutback or saving. Planning for the hospitals to be built was not complete and contracts could not be let in fiscal 1954.

[4] Unobligated balances of $18.5 million were sufficient to cover the necessary expenditures.

[5] Although reductions in amounts for the purpose of liquidating contract authority are not normally real cuts, this one was apparently real because of the issue of a "freeze order" on construction.

[6] A real cut, but need for funds for this program had decreased.

[7] Expenditures slated for liquidation of contract authority depend entirely on actual amounts committed.

[8] Costs of transporting mail are fixed almost completely by rates and by volume.

[9] Expenditures for this item do not come out of the Federal Treasury, but are made from foreign credits. The reduction did not save any federal funds.

Source: Senate Appropriations Committee, *Appropriation Acts and Reports*, 83d Cong., 1st Sess. (1953), and *Comparison of Original Estimates and Revised Estimates, 1954*, by Departments, in Regular Bills (Committee Print)[c] 83d Cong. 2d Sess. (1954).

82d Congress during the Second Session. A similar situation may be found in a review of the Eisenhower revisions for Mutual Security and Defense.[6] The precise effects of the revised estimates on appropriations for the Department of Defense are most difficult to determine. An analysis is muddied by many factors, and most significant being the following:

1. The costs of the Korean War, formerly separated from the regular Defense appropriation bill, were included in the revised requests. This made it appear that there was actually an increase for many items, especially for the Army, which was not actually the case.
2. Total requests for 1953, $51,400,000,000, were about 25 percent greater than the Truman requests for 1954.
3. The total reductions proposed in the revised estimates were $4,900,000,000, of which $4,800,000,000 consisted of reductions in the Air Force. This is distorted by the inclusion of Korean War costs. The Navy was reduced $1,700,000,000 while the Army was increased $1,600,000,000. Nevertheless, the major cut was in the Air Force, and there was a real question as to what the effects would be.

There is no way that analysis can remove the uncertainties stemming from the first two items above. However, the huge size of the Air Force reduction would indicate that this might be a fruitful area to analyze.

The Eisenhower budget request for the Department of Defense was $35,800,000,000, or nearly $5,000,000,000 below the $40,700,-000,000 requested by Truman.[7] Virtually all of the reduction consisted of Air Force cuts which amounted to $4,800,000,000, or from $16,100,000,000 to $11,300,000,000. The effects of this appropriations cutback were highly disputed. A detailed examination of this issue is beyond the scope of this study, but we should survey it briefly in an attempt to assess the Eisenhower budget as compared with the Truman budget.

The Truman budget contemplated a 143-wing Air Force to be achieved by 1955. General Hoyt S. Vandenberg, Chief of Staff of the Air Force under Truman, declared that the reductions in appropriations would prevent the attainment of this goal on schedule.[8]

Secretary of Air, Harold Talbott, disputed this, declaring that the reductions could be accomplished by reducing "lead time."[9] But the reduction in lead time was not the only issue. The administration also asserted that reductions would be made in the noncombat phases of the Air Force program in an attempt to squeeze out waste, or, as one wag put it, to "get more bang for a buck."[10] General Vandenberg asserted that there would be substantial harm in these reductions and proposed an additional $1,400,000,000 for "the achievement of a 143-wing program at the earliest practicable date."[11] Thus it is virtually impossible to determine whether reduction represented: (1) a cutback in Air Force strength; (2) elimination or nonessential expenditures; or (3) merely a postponement of spending authority. One thing is certain, however. All of the $4,800,000,000 reduction was not real in the sense that it cut either strength or nonessential programs. The fact that much of the administration's defense of the reduction was based on mere postponement of expenditures would suggest that a large proportion of the reduction was not real.

Again, when we compare the Eisenhower reductions below the Truman requests for the whole Defense Establishment compared with the reductions the 82d Congress made in Truman's previous budget, the similarity in over-all cuts is striking:

Defense appropriations reductions of 82d Congress below Truman requests for the fiscal year 1952–53................$4,800,000,000
Eisenhower reductions in appropriations requests for Defense below amounts received by Truman for fiscal year 1953–54...........
....$4,900,000,000

CONCLUSIONS

We can summarize the new administration's actions on the 1954 Truman budget very briefly. It did, indeed, reduce the Truman requests, but it apparently did so mostly by (1) predicting congressional action on a Truman budget and using this as a basis for submitting the revised requests, and (2) cutting appropriations requests to make "paper" or unreal reductions. Our analysis of the revised requests is naturally imperfect, but further evidence that this was the course of the administration's methods is borne out by comparing actual expenditures with Truman budget estimates for the fiscal years 1953 and 1954:

Fiscal Year	Truman Budget Estimate of Expenditures	Actual Expenditures	Difference
1953	$85,400,000,000	$74,300,000,000	$11,100,000,000
1954	78,600,000,000	67,600,000,000	11,000,000,000

The fact that expenditures for 1953 (based on appropriations enacted by the 82d Congress, 2d Session) were almost precisely the same amount under the estimates as were expenditures for 1954 (based on revised appropriations requests) bears out our conclusions. Thus the administration not only failed to advocate or introduce new methods of helping Congress to control expenditures; evidence indicates that it actually used the work of Congress itself as a yardstick for its own proposals.

Perhaps these things were done to mark time until the new administration could get its bearings. Certainly it had to move quickly in order to get the revised requests submitted in time for congressional consideration. Nevertheless, it was grossly misleading for Republican orators and advertisements to trumpet their "accomplishments" to the nation's voters after having used, to a large extent, the work of the Democratic 82d Congress as a guide-on.

CONGRESSIONAL LEGERDEMAIN

We turn now to the action of the 83d Congress, First Session (1953) on the revised appropriations requests for the fiscal year 1953–54 in order to determine whether the changes in party leadership of Congress brought in its wake any changes in congressional methods in the appropriations process.

Returning to Senator Bridges' statement, we find that, in addition to the $9,300,000,000 billion cuts made by Eisenhower in the Truman requests, "Congress effected a further reduction of $3,454,274,596, producing a combined reduction of $12,712,-201,500."[12] Let us take a look at this $3,500,000,000 in additional cuts. These are revealed in Table 9, along with the total amounts which were not real savings.

As shown in Table 9, $2,200,000,000 or approximately two-thirds of the total amount of savings claimed in the Bridges statement as having been made in addition to reductions proposed in the revised estimates were unreal. This fact should not be construed as criticism of Congress for making this type of reduction in all cases. There was certainly no good reason for postponing appropriations for the civil service retirement fund, nor, for that matter, for reappropriating past appropriations rather than letting them lapse in favor of new appropriations. But is not necessarily unsound policy to refuse money requests in excess of single fiscal year requirements, unless future spending authority is necessary

Table 9

SUMMARY OF CLAIMED AND UNREAL SAVINGS MADE BY
CONGRESS ON EISENHOWER APPROPRIATION
REQUESTS FOR FISCAL YEAR 1954

(Millions of Dollars)

AppropriationsBill	Total Claimed Savings	Total Unreal Savings
First Independent Offices....................	441.5	402.9
Second Independent Offices.................	358.6	416.6
Department of Interior......................	57.5	28.7
Department of Agriculture.................	(14.6) (increase)	—
Departments of State, Justice, Commerce....	185.6	130.6
Departments of Treasury and Post Office.....	5.0	—
Departments of Labor and Health, Education and Welfare...........................	11.5	21.4
Civil Functions, Department of Army........	58.6	53.6
District of Columbia......................	(3.9)	—
Legislative and Judiciary..................	17.6	—
Department of Defense.....................	1,400.1	522.0
Mutual Security...........................	607.4	607.4
1954 Supplemental........................	305.4	—
Drought Relief (supplemental)..............	20.0	—
Total............................	3,454.3	2,183.2

Explanation of Unreal Savings

The following reductions were unreal because they represented either (a) reappropriations, (b) mere postponement of providing funds for fixed obligations, or (c) items for which funds could not possibly be spent because of insufficient plans or unavailability of goods:

First Independent Offices

1. Payments to civil service retirement and disability fund (normal cost)—$176,100,000.
2. Payment to civil service retirement and disability fund (interest) —$192,000,000.
3. Payment to civil service retirement and disability fund for increase in annuities—$27,600,000.
4. Annual contributions, Public Housing Administration—$7,600,-000.

Table 9 (Continued)

Second Independent Offices

1. Operating expenses, Atomic Energy Commission—$38,200,000.
2. Compensation and pensions, Veterans Administration—$253,-700,000.
3. Readjustment benefits, Veterans Administration—$124,700,000.

Interior

1. Construction and rehabilitation, Bureau of Reclamation—$28,-700,000.

Departments of State, Justice and Commerce

1. Salaries and expenses, State Department—$15,600,000.
2. Ship construction, maritime activities, Department of Commerce (liquidation of contract authority)—$5,000,000.
3. Operating differential subsidies, maritime activities, Department of Commerce—$45,000,000.
4. Federal aid highways, Bureau of Public Roads, Department of Commerce—$65,000,000.

Labor and Health, Education and Welfare

1. Grants to States, Bureau of Employment Security—$21,500,000.

Civil Functions, Department of the Army

1. Construction, rivers and harbors and flood control—$53,600,000.

Mutual Security

Total unreal reductions in all items—$607,400,000.

Department of Defense

Total unreal reduction in all items—$522,000,000, as follows:

Office of the Secretary of Defense

1. Retired pay—$10,000,000.
2. Reserve tools and facilities—$250,000,000.

Department of the Army

1. Procurement and production—$100,000,000.
2. Reserve personnel requirements—$17,000,000.

Department of the Navy

1. Procurement, Marine Corps—$100,000,000.
2. Ordnance for new construction (liquidation of contract authorization)—$45,000,000.

Source: Senate Committee on Appropriations, *Appropriation Acts and Reports* (Committee Print), 83d Cong., 1st Sess. (1953), and *Comparison of Original Estimates and Revised Estimates, 1954, by Departments, in Regular Bills* (Committee Print), 83d Cong., 2d Sess. (1954).

to permit planning or to get plans underway by negotiating contracts. Nevertheless, the practice of making unreal reductions which are lumped in with total reductions in appropriation requests is a phenomenon which leads to much confusion about what precisely Congress has done with respect to the requests.

Neither the new administration nor the new Congress under Republican leadership made any changes in congressional appropriating procedures. The reductions proposed by the new administration were based on the actions of the previous Congress, and the cuts made by the new Congress itself were mostly unreal, paper savings. Thus the change in party leadership made no difference so far as the problem of congressional control of expenditures is concerned. However, the review of a budget prepared by one administration, revised by another, and passed on by a Congress controlled by the same political party as the new administration, reveals the degree to which budgetary appropriations procedures may be employed for political purposes.

Chapter 9

Success by Standards

All the preceding chapters in Part II have dealt with congressional attempts to control expenditures which have generally been frustrating and inadequate. We have seen the appeal to legislative conservatism, meat-axe cuts, and attacks on overhead as practices substituted for analysis. We have also seen the political ramifications in federal construction expenditures and the use of legerdemain and manipulation of budgetary and appropriations figures. Nevertheless, we must not paint the picture of congressional expenditures control totally black. In this chapter, we shall review what is probably the best general method for ascertaining the consequences of appropriations actions, the establishment of legislative standards for appropriations.

Obviously, to the extent that basic authorizing legislation can set standards which will permit Congress to know precisely the consequences of any appropriations actions it may take in future years, the problem of congressional control disappears. Although the use of such standards is subject to certain limitations, much of the search for methods of better congressional control of spending is actually a search for better methods of establishing adequate legislative standards. But the nature of legislation for, and administration of, federal programs is usually such that adequate standards cannot be set. To take an extreme example, Congress might set for the Department of Defense the "standard" of "the best possible defense for the least amount of money." The problem is not found in a lack of standards but in ascertaining to what degree the standards are being met.

Congress should, of course, set as precise standards as possible in its authorizing legislation so that Members can know with maximum possible certainty the consequences of any amount that may be appropriated. In this regard, it must beware of creating a new obstacle—inflexibility in the authorizing legislation. This difficulty, however, can be offset by permitting the administering agency to develop the standards within the framework of legislative criteria, with periodic review of the law (by cutoff dates). Our purpose is not to restrict administrative discretion but rather to provide standards capable of permitting Congress to know as nearly as possible the effects of any amount it appropriates for a particular program. The fact that precisely ascertainable standards are impossible over such a wide range of programs (i.e., defense, foreign aid, atomic energy, and the post office) should not preclude Congress from employing them in areas where they can be used. For ascertainable standards not only permit Congress greater money control but also facilitate the administration of a program with a maximum of fairness and objectivity and a minimum of abuse and poor judgment.

General Standards

In reviewing congressional action on money requests, we find that legislative standards are often employed in the voting of funds for grants to States and for subsidy programs. These standards vary in their effectiveness.

The simplest legislative standards are those which make the payment of funds automatic when certain conditions are met, a selfimposed restriction by Congress on its own powers of appropriation. For example, laws which set the rates of veterans' pensions determine the amounts which, morally at least, Congress must appropriate. Another such example is represented by an appropriation item for "Grants to States for Public Assistance." The Bureau of Public Assistance in the Department of Health, Education, and Welfare is charged with the administration of four programs of federal financial aid to the fifty States, the District of Columbia, Puerto Rico, and the Virgin Islands. These programs consist of grants for old-age assistance, aid to dependent children, aid to the blind, and aid to the permanently and totally disabled. To a large extent the States, within the framework of the federal Social Security legislation, determine their own aid programs, and the federal government is enjoined by law to match the costs of the program according to an established formula. Thus ascertainable standards are set to such a degree that even Congress can exercise very little control over any appropriation for public assistance. Only by changing the basic legislation could these amounts be changed. There are some variables and uncertainties, but the overwhelming amount of each annual appropriation is predetermined by the programs of the fifty-three jurisdictions entitled to the grants.[1]

Legislative standards for appropriations also permit ascertainable results of spending authority in the case of the federal-aid highway program administered by the Bureau of Public Roads in the Department of Commerce. The importance of considering the appropriations process for the highway program stems both from the way which it operates on the basis of adequate standards and from the way Congress loses control over the amounts to be appropriated. Grants to specific States, under the program, must follow a specified formula as set forth in the authorizing legislation. This formula takes into account both geographic area and population size and fixes a policy of allocation not subject to to administrative discretion. Hence Congress may appropriate funds for the program with precise information about the use of the funds as in the case of the Public Assistance Program, and the federal-aid highway appropriation is treated as a binding commitment. Congress apparently feels that once the Bureau of Public Roads makes a commitment to a State, based on the authorizing legislation, it must honor that commitment by providing the necessary funds.

Briefly, the process of carrying out the program follows this pattern. Congress enacts a federal-aid highway act authorizing federal funds for highway purposes. On the strength of the authorization, the Bureau of Public Roads makes allotments to the States on the basis of a formula which has been prescribed by Congress in the act. The States agree to match the federal funds and proceed to let contracts for the work. After the work is completed and accepted, the federal share of the cost statement is presented to the Bureau of Public Roads. The amount appropriated by Congress for a particular fiscal year is based on the amount of the cost statements that the Bureau of Public Roads anticipates will be presented during that period.

A widely held conclusion among Members of Congress that the authorization constitutes a prior commitment of federal funds which commits Congress to subsequent appropriation is a source of concern to various Members of Congress.[2] Legally, one legislature cannot bind another.[3] However, Congress apparently does not consider the legal side of these appropriations, but, rather, the "moral" side; that is, the fact that the States have completed the highway work according to the expectations of the legislation and agreements made by the Bureau of Public Roads based on such legislation. The rationale for Congress' abdicating annual control over the amounts it appropriates for highways lies in the need for advance planning of such construction by the States. If the State highway departments do not know the amount of money they will receive until the year it is appropriated, they do not have sufficient time to develop their over-all plans. By enabling the Bureau of Public Roads to make allocations on the basis of the legislative authorization, the States can proceed with their planning with knowledge of how much will be paid by the federal government.

Another appropriation item for which Congress binds itself to appropriate in accordance with commitments made in conformance with known standards is "conservation and use of agricultural land resources." This is the Agricultural Conservation Payments program, administered by what was formerly called the Production and Marketing Administration. The program is primarily one of making direct subsidy payments to farmers for carrying out approved soil conservation practices. The item is not to be confused with the appropriation for the Soil Conservation Service, an agency providing farmers with technical help. For our purposes, however, the importance of the ACP item does not lie in the degree to which Congress binds itself to appropriate for past commitments. Rather, we shall concern ourselves with the adequacy of standards in the establishment of the level at which future commitments can be made.

Let us consider the standards by which commitments are made under the ACP program. It is formulated under the provisions of sections 7 to 17, inclusive, of the Soil Conservation and Domestic Allotment Act, approved February 29, 1936, as amended. The purposes of that Act to assist farmers in carrying out conservation practices include restoring and improving soil fertility, reducing erosion caused by wind and water, and conserving water on land. To achieve these ends, the Agricultural Conservation program offers assistance to individual farmers and ranchers in all of the fifty States, Puerto Rico, and the Virgin Islands for carrying out approved soil-building and soil-and water-conserving practices on their farms.

The practices for which assistance is offered generally fall into four major classes:

1. Constructing, such as terracing, leveling land, and building dams;
2. Establishing pastures of perennial grasses and other permanent cover;
3. Growing annual cover crops, such as winter or annual legumes; and
4. Applying minerals such as lime and phosphate to pasture and hayland sods.

Rates of assistance to farmers for approved practices vary by practices and by States and areas to make the most effective use of available funds. The average rate of assistance for all practices is less than one-half the cost of performing the practice with the farmer bearing the balance of the cost and supplying the labor necessary to carry out the practice. Assistance is available in the form of materials and services furnished to the farmer for carrying out approved practices or in the form of cash as partial reimbursement to farmers who have carried them out at their own expense. Materials and services are obtained through local private sources where practicable.[4]

While the ACP program is thus one in which there would appear to be ample standards for Congress to reach a decision on the level of commitments, it is difficult to ascertain the intricacies of administration. A Member of Congress can get all sorts of breakdowns on the purposes for which the funds are allocated, the types of practices to be subsidized, and the extent of the subsidy for each, where the money is spent by State and even by county. Thus, had Congress desired to stop subsidies for nonpermanent types of practices, it could have done so with a proviso in the appropriation law. It could have eliminated the whole program or any part thereof. The same was not true with respect to the degree of efficiency of administration. Members had little information for determining if the program could be administered at less cost or whether more administrative funds might have been worth while in terms of increased services.

Specific Standards

Congress has employed general standards for considering subsidy programs, but it has also developed very specific standards so that the precise effects of any amount appropriated for an item can be known. An excellent example of such a program was the one for school construction in the so-called "federally-affected" areas. The purpose of the school construction program, authorized by Public Law 815, 81st Congress, was to provide federal aid to local school districts near military reservations and other areas impacted by population increases caused by defense plants or defense installations. It was administered by the U. S. Office of Education. The basic reason for the program was that some school districts were expected to provide for the education of children of parents who lived on and/or worked on federal property which was not subject to local taxation. In some of the smaller communities, this often meant a doubling or tripling of enrollment without corresponding increases in taxable property, either residential or commercial. Thus federal aid was extended to such areas to provide the necessary additional school buildings.[5]

The program went further, however. In some areas, defense plants would hire thousands of new workers with school-age children. They would live in trailers or double-up on housing so that taxable property did not increase in the same ratio as the increase in the number of children to be educated. Federal aid was given for children of these workers, also, but not as much as for others.

A rather ingenious formula was devised for determining how much federal aid a local school district should receive. Generally, the formula took into account the degree to which the locality should share the burden of increased enrollment. For example, it provided more help for children of parents living on and working on federal property than for children of parents living off but working on such property. The program extended even less aid for children of parents, such as those working in newly created defense plants, who lived and worked on private, taxable property. In addition, the law set standards for determining actual needs for school buildings and other factors. The formula took these into account in determining a local school district's "entitlement."

But the precise nature of the standards did not end here. Priorities based on need were also established. For instance, if a total of 100 districts qualified for entitlements totaling $100,000,000, all were ranked, with those in greatest need at the top of the priority list. If Congress then appropriated the entire $100,000,000, all would get their entitlements enabling them to construct their desired buildings. If, however, Congress appropriated only $85,000,000, the full entitlements went to all possible districts, but those at the bottom of the priority list had to wait. Thus Congress was assured that any reduction it voted would be effected in a way least damaging to real needs.

It is difficult to conceive of a program designed to give Congress a more precise appropriations control. With known standards, priorities, published lists of districts affected, their entitlements, and priorities, one could almost say that this type of program organization should be emulated wherever possible. The legislation provided aid for schools in federally-affected areas. Qualifications and amounts were worked out which gave greatest weight to increases in the number of school children of parents who both lived and worked on federal property. Children of parents who *either* lived *or* worked on federal property were also counted, but less weight was given in the formula for them. Even less weight was given to children whose parents neither lived nor worked on federal property, but these were considered if it could be shown that they had come into the district because of defense activities.

The legislation directed the Commissioner of Education, in the event that appropriations were insufficient to meet all qualified applications, to issue regulations prescribing "the order of priority in which approved applications shall be certified for payment. . . ." According to the House committee report, these regulations were to give priorities "on the basis of the 'relative urgency of the need' of such projects."[8]

The U. S. Office of Education employed a fair and simple method of computing priority "indexes" within the criteria set forth above. The priortiy for a particular school district was arrived at on the basis of the total number of students, the normal capacity of available facilities—the difference being the number of unhoused pupils. The number of federal pupils eligible for payment was also computed. The percentage of federally-connected pupils and the percentage of unhoused pupils were then figured. The priority index number was the percentage by which it was necessary to multiply the percentage of federally-connected pupils, the results of which, when added to the percentage of federally-connected pupils, would add up to a sum equal to the percentage of unhoused pupils.

With standards such as these, Congress can be assured of the consequences of any amount it may appropriate for the program. The agency will request the total amounts for which it has approved payment on the basis of known standards. But, with the priority arrangements worked out in addition, Congress can know that any reduction it may make in the appropriation will affect only the lowest priority projects. Were Congress able to have such standards before it in considering all appropriations, there would be virtually no problem of not knowing the consequences of its money enactments. Though this is impossible, it represents a goal which should be sought after in all its authorizing legislation.

the state of which when added to the experience of laterally,
to theoretical. could add no possible equal to any relevance
of reduced ratio.

Well, that first and there, Congress can be assured to the
consequences of my freedom in favor and opinion to the process.
I embrace with approval total annuities for which is not reduced increase on the basis of hiatus accuracy? In reply to the
other commercial a disposition should no. I improve sanctions
that may prevent it may make to the application we will need
into the better priority supplied. We to the we able to have such
specialists favor duty transferring all the perpetration shall would
the victory. It is not of its out knowing the other success
so on a sure thing. Through the reflex which it was take a failure
which should assure a state in the permanent representation.

Potential Improvements in Control

Chapter 10

Changing the Rules

In considering the degree to which Congress acts on appropriations with knowledge of the consequences, we have reviewed the congressional spending role, procedures, facilities and the techniques for dealing with money questions. We have also viewed some of the political ramifications of the appropriations process. We turn now to an analysis of the most popular recommendations for improvements in the handling of appropriations. The two major proposals for "changing the rules" are the omnibus, or consolidated, appropriations bill, rather than ten or twelve separate bills, and the item veto empowering the President to veto parts of an appropriation bill without nullifying the entire measure. This chapter will deal with these two recommendations, and the following chapter will consider proposals for enlarging congressional staff aids to help Members better analyze the budget requests.

THE CONSOLIDATED APPROPRIATION BILL

Appropriations measures are generally of three types: (1) regular appropriation bills, for which the budgetary estimates are presented at the beginning of a session, (2) supplemental bills, for which the estimates are not submitted until late in the session, and (3) deficiency bills, which make appropriations for a current fiscal year, after regular and supplemental bills have already been passed, usually the year before.

One of the most often mentioned proposals for improvement of the appropriations process is to have Congress consider all *regular* appropriations items in a single bill, in effect, lumping together some eleven or twelve regular bills into one omnibus measure. Senator Harry Byrd, Democrat of Virginia, took the lead in advocating the proposal, introducing resolutions to this effect in the 80th, 81st, 82d, 83d, 84th, 85th and 86th Congresses. It was passed twice by the Senate, in the 81st Congress and in the 83d Congress.[1] The House of Representatives has never acted on the Byrd resolution, but Rep. Clarence Cannon, Chairman of the House Appropriations Committee, announced on May 26, 1949 that his committee would submit the annual appropriations in one consolidated bill beginning with the Second Session of the 81st Congress. Mr. Cannon said that "no special enactments or change in rules are necessary in order to provide for the consolidated budget or its consideration in either House."[2]

Proponents of the omnibus bill declared that it would:

1. Facilitate observance of the recommended ceiling on expenditures.
2. Permit a comparison of total appropriations with the latest estimates for total receipts for the coming year.
3. Focus responsibility for any increase in the public debt.
4. Offer a method of financial retrenchment.
5. Enable Congress to act more intelligently on budget requests.
6. Make the pruning of agency estimates more orderly and less haphazard.
7. Offset the pleas of pressure groups.
8. Permit Congress to see the budget picture as a whole.
9. Probably reduce the number of deficiency and supplemental appropriations bills.[3]

On January 9, 1950, Mr. Cannon told the House of Representatives that by using the one-package bill:

Appropriations will be more carefully processed; duplications, overlapping and conflicts will be reconciled; legislative items will be eliminated; logrolling will be impracticable as all the cards will be on the table at one time and any attempted trades will be too apparent to withstand the light of publicity; the entire expenditures for the year will be submitted in one figure simultaneously with an authoritative estimate of the national income; deficit financing will be discouraged, as a last opportunity will be afforded for reconsideration in the subcommittees of the entire bill with a view of bringing annual expenditures within the annual revenues of the Government; and the bill will have been passed and all annual appropriations enacted before the end of the fiscal year, obviating the need for the usual continuing resolutions and permitting adjournment of Congress much earlier than heretofore.[4]

Thus in 1950, Congress tried the single-package appropriation bill. The method was used only once, however, and Congress has not gone back to it.

Dr. Galloway has called the 1950 omnibus bill a tour de force.

Writing in retrospect, he declared:

> Theretofore the supply bills had gone through the 28 stages of the legislative process in piecemeal fashion, each bill being handled separately by different subcommittees, with little or no consideration of their interrelationships or systematic allocation of public revenues among governmental functions and services. Each of the money bills had been considered individually at the committee and floor stages. Lack of over-all control encouraged deficiency and supplemental requests for funds, which still further weakened congressional control. The President submitted a unified budget to Congress, which broke it up into bits and pieces. In 1950, however, appropriations were merged into one bill which reduced the President's estimates by more than two billion dollars and which was ready for his signature two full months ahead of the budget authorization completion date in 1949.

Dr. Galloway conceded that "there were rumblings of dissatisfaction with the new procedure in both Houses." With respect to these, however, he said only that there were "conflicting claims" and that "some members disliked [it] because it impeded the flow of federal funds . . . for favored projects." This he countered by quoting Mr. Cannon, who said that the consolidated bill was opposed by "every predatory lobbyist, every pressure group seeking to get its hands into the . . . Treasury, every bureaucrat seeking to extend his empire. . . ." and that "one weakness of our form of government" is that "Congressmen reap political benefit in the form of votes by getting federal money spent in their respective bailiwicks."[5] In the latter respect, Mr. Cannon may have been right. Certainly there has never been any assertion that Mr. Cannon ever injured himself politically by virtue of his being Chairman of the House Appropriations Committee and his ability to get large sums spent for river improvements in his Missouri district, which includes a large part of the lower Missouri River and borders on the Mississippi River.

In view of all the statements in favor of the consolidated bill, one naturally wonders what the arguments are against it. As we shall see, there is more logic to the opposition than has heretofore been implied. There are both positive reasons for using separate bills and negative reasons for overruling arguments in favor of the omnibus approach. Let us consider the latter first.

The most prevalent point raised in favor of the omnibus bill is that it allows Congress and the public to view the budgetary picture as a whole. This relates to criticisms that the present process is "piecemeal," that it "breaks up the budget into bits and pieces" and that a consolidated bill would permit an over-all comparison of total appropriations with total receipts, making pruning more orderly and less haphazard. This position, however, ignores four pertinent facts: (1) the budget document already gives the over-all picture, containing both appropriations and expenditures estimates, (2) the consolidated bill, on the other hand, cannot possibly give an over-all picture, (3) expenditures are not the same as appropriations, and (4) the only procedural difference between the omnibus and the separate bill approach is that under the former, the committee holds up the separate bills until all are ready for reporting. The net effect is to report some twelve bills simultaneously in the form of chapters in a single measure.

With respect to giving an "over-all" view, let us look at the appropriations for the fiscal year 1951, where Congress made use of the single bill. According to a recent Senate report:

> The one-package bill for 1951 was enacted into law by September 6, providing about $34 billion, of which 4 billion for foreign aid was added by the Senate. Immediately behind it, the first supplemental for 1951 was enacted into law on September 27, providing for 17 billion, and then before the session adjourned in December the second supplemental for 1951 was passed, providing for almost 20 billion additional. Then in this year, the third supplemental for 1951 and the fourth supplemental for 1951 were enacted in May and June, providing for 400 million and for over 6 billion additional. Therefore, the one-package for 1951 gave the Congress and the public a picture, not of 100 per cent of the 1951 funds, but actually of only 43 per cent of those funds.[6]

The picture painted above may understate the percentage of funds which can be covered in a single bill, for 1950 was the year of the outbreak of the Korean War and hence not a normal year. Yet it is true that there are generally large sums included in supplemental and deficiency bills as well as permanent appropriations which would not and could not be covered in any omnibus bill.

Does the consolidated bill save time? Dr. Galloway pointed out that the consolidated bill was passed in 1950 by August 4, two full months before the comparable date of passage of the last appropriation bill in 1949. This comparison is faulty on at least three counts: (1) 1949 was not an election year, as was 1950, when Congress was anxious to get home, (2) the comparison was too narrow, not being made with several years. For example, all 1946 bills were passed by July 3; 1947 bills, by July 26; 1948 bills, by July 31; and 1949 bills, by June 30,[7] and (3) Dr. Galloway failed to take account of the fact that in 1950 *all* agencies had to wait until the last bill was approved, whereas under the separate bill system, many of them, having had their funds bills passed previously, could proceed with planning without having to wait for the others.

Does the consolidated bill lead to greater economy? Dr. Galloway pointed out that $2,000,000,000 had been cut from the budget requests by the consolidated bill. While this was a somewhat larger cut than that imposed by Congress for the two preceding years, the $2,000,000,000 compares with cuts of $4,000,000,000 made the following year (1951 measures, funds for fiscal year 1952), $8,500,000,000 the next year and reductions of $12,000,000,000 in 1954 funds passed in 1953. This does not necessarily mean that separate bills result in greater reductions, but it indicates that the consolidated bill process does not, of itself, produce or even facilitate reductions.

The main disadvantage of the consolidated bill is the problem it presents to Members of Congress who are not members of the Appropriations Committees. Normally, an appropriations bill goes through a subcommittee to the full committee and is reported when ready. Individual Members may then review the bill and select points on which they differ with the committee for floor action. This is possible in the case of individual bills. Even though markups are held in secret sessions and committee recommendations are not known until the bill is reported, there is still ample time for study. But in the case of a consolidated bill, the Member has no idea of what the recommendations are likely to be until the sum total of all recommendations included in the equivalent of twelve bills descend, in an avalanche, on him at one time. By the time all bills are held up in committee until the last one is ready, it is late in the session, with tremendous pressures built up to rush through the bill with only a few days' study of the hundreds of items involved.

The main value of committee study is to save time for individual Members of Congress and permit them to devote themselves to the items for which they feel the committee did not recommend proper amounts. The value of the committee is lost if there is not sufficient time to review its recommendations and to study particular items before the general floor debate takes place. One therefore wonders whether it might not possibly be that the cursory attention given by individual Members in examining appropriation matters under the consolidated system is the reason for its popularity in some quarters—especially by those who prefer that Congress deal only in "policy" and not delve into "details."

Yet, as a matter of fact, the demise of the consolidated approach was brought about not by individual Members but by those sitting on Appropriations Committees. After the 1950 experience, the House Appropriations Committee voted 31 to 18 against continuing the consolidated system, every subcommittee chairman of the Senate committee issued a statement condemning it, and the Bureau of the Budget opposed it unless a provision for an item veto were included. In backing up their opposition, the Senate subcommittee chairman said, among other things, that the bill had proved to be bulky, unmanageable, and impracticable. Originating in the House of Representatives, it placed legislative burdens on both branches of Congress which became intolerable. The chairmen also charged that it encouraged meat-axe cuts rather than selective reductions; opened the way to legislative riders (the Bridges-Byrd amendment attached to the consolidated bill, discussed in Chapter V, was a meat-axe cut in the form of a legislative rider) ; delayed the Senate subcommittees by compelling them to wait for the House to pass all bills; and consumed a longer period of time for action, delaying passage of many single bills. For all these reasons, it rendered economies more difficult to achieve.[8]

In summary, the omnibus bill is actually a hindrance to the appropriations process.

THE ITEM VETO

Proposals to extend the veto power of the President by giving him authority to veto individual items in appropriations bills involves fundamental and far-reaching considerations affecting the basic power relationships between the executive and legislative branches of the government. Well over 100 measures providing for an item veto have been introduced since 1873. These have differed in scope and detail. Some applied to all appropriations bills; others, to general appropriations bills. Some were confined to rivers and harbors bills. Several would have allowed the President to reduce as well as veto individual items. Some would have permitted the vetoed items to be restored by a majority of both houses of Congress; others would have retained the two-thirds requirement for item vetoes as well as for general vetoes. The only time the item veto principle has been subjected to a vote in either House was in 1883.[9]

Background

The origins of the veto power itself are too well known to treat at length here. Suffice it to say that the colonies chafed under the veto power of the King or the Royal Governors, which acted as a severe check on the legislative assemblies. Indeed, the first two grievances set forth in the Declaration of Independence were "He had refused his assent to laws. . . . He has forbidden his governors to pass laws." All semblance of an executive veto of any kind was abolished immediately after the Revolution, both in the State and National Governments.

The weaknesses of "headless" government soon became apparent under the Articles of Confederation, and, despite some misgivings, a limited veto power was given the Chief Executive under the Constitution. Following the lead of the Federal Government, the States gradually restored the veto power to their executives. It was not until the period of the Civil War, however, that the item veto came into being, first in the Provisional Constitution of the Confederate States. Then it was adopted by Georgia in 1865 and by Texas the following year. Since the Civil War, nearly every new State admitted to the Union adopted the item veto as did many of the older ones. There are now thirty-nine States which extend to their governors the power of the item veto on appropriation bills.[10]

As the States adopted the item veto, agitation began for a similar provision in the federal Constitution. The practice of passing riders on appropriations bills induced many Presidents, beginning with Grant, to favor such a provision, and the issue has been debated from that time to the present. President Eisenhower, in his January, 1959, State of the Union Message, recommended the item veto on both appropriations and authorization bills.[11]

The Case for the Item Veto

The most common arguments advanced in favor of the item veto are that it would:

1. Reduce extravagance in public expenditures. The President would be personally responsible for economy and efficiency in his administration.

2. Discourage "pork barrel" appropriations.
3. Curb logrolling.
4. *Restore* to the President his veto power on legislation. Legislative provisions are often added to appropriations bills, thus coercing the President to suffer measures to become law which he does not approve, or to incur the risk of stopping the wheels of government by vetoing an appropriations bill.
5. Expedite completion of legislative programs by permitting review of vetoed items rather than entire vetoed bills.
6. Be feasible because it works in thirty-nine States and governors in those States which do not have it think it would be very helpful.

The executive power of the item veto would probably not increase expenditures since the power is purely negative with respect to appropriations. President Grant declared that providing the Executive with such power "would protect the public against the many abuses and waste of public moneys which creep into appropriations bills . . ." and that it "would check extravagant legislation."[12] One early student of the veto power, Edward C. Mason, stated that "The very least that could be said is that the charge would not increase the expenditure of the government, and in all probability it would diminish it."[13] Another early student, Calvin P. Godfrey, declared that

especially true is it, that public expenditures of a sensible and frugal character never can be so well assured if there is lacking this power to excise items of appropriations . . . the taxpayer's interest needs to be as carefully guarded in the spending as in the gathering. And it becomes the State first to provide a means to such an end. The simplest and plainest and surest one is a veto of appropriation items. For by it public income and outgo can be rationally balanced and easily so maintained. Present economies can be more scrupulously enforced, legitimate demands more easily met. A complete policy of retrenchment can be announced confidently and adhered to faithfully.[14]

Closely related to the money-saving argument is the assertion that the item veto would curb "pork barrel" appropriations. President Cleveland recognized what he considered to be a danger which results from collusive appropriations for local projects when he said:

Appropriation bills for the support of the Government are defaced by items and provisions to meet private ends, and it is freely asserted by responsible and experienced parties that a bill appropriating money for public internal improvement would fail to meet with

PART III. *Potential Improvements*

favor unless it contained items more for local and private advantage than for public benefit.[15]

Another argument in favor of the item veto relating to the proposition that it would reduce expenditures is the claim that it would curb logrolling. This term refers to the practice, implicit or explicit, of a Member of Congress agreeing to support anothers' pet project in return for the other's support of his, thus, in total, building up a bill including a great many projects not justified in the national interest. "Somebody else has to take the broad view, to look after the nation or the State, while they [the legislators] are absorbed with Buncombe County or Podunk," Charles A. Beard has said. "And this somebody is getting to be more and more the directly [sic] elect of all the people."[16]

A more substantive argument, pertaining to the constitutional power relationship of the Executive to Congress rather than personal preferences as to the merits of less spending and construction projects of a local nature, is the assertion that the item veto is necessary to restore to the President his veto power. This power, according to the argument, implies that the President shall be free to give effect to his independent judgment upon the merits of bills which come before him for approval or disapproval. Such independent judgment cannot now in all cases be exercised by the President. Bills presented for his action sometimes comprise two or more unrelated subjects. He may favor one but oppose the other, so he cannot deal with the two subjects separately upon their merits. Whatever his action, it applies to and affects both subjects alike. Thus, by joining in a single bill diverse subjects of varying degrees of merit and requiring action by the President upon the bill as a whole, he is deprived of the power of independent judgment, and coerced into either accepting that of which his judgment disapproves or defeating that which he believes wise and necessary. The resulting evils cited are (1) the practical powerlessness of the President to exert any effective restraining influence upon general appropriations bills, and (2) the frequent enactment of measures opposed by the President by attaching them as "riders" to a general appropriations bills whose passage is usually indispensable to the operation of government, and whose acceptance by the President is therefore practically compulsory.[17]

The proposition that the item veto would expedite legislative programs is based on the premise that if the President did veto an entire appropriations bill, the whole bill would again run the gamut of Congress rather than the particular item to which the President objected. The final argument, namely, that the item veto has worked successfully in the States, assumes the comparability of legislative-executive relationships in the States to that of the federal government.

The Case Against the Item Veto

The item veto has never reached the stage which evokes much verbal opposition. Nevertheless, arguments that have been raised against it can be listed. Opponents assert that such a veto would:

1. Lessen the responsibility of Congress for appropriations.
2. Unduly increase the influence of the Executive by taking away the only effective power the Congress now has over the President (apart from impeachment) and substituting the President's purely personal opinion for that of Congress in legislative matters, which would defeat the legislative intent of Congress to discharge its duty to each and all.
3. Be entirely unnecessary.
4. Be an uncertain grant of power—definition of such expressions as "disapprove of any item," "reduce," etc., have caused considerable concern in State courts.

Lessening congressional responsibility. The argument that the item veto would lessen the responsibility of Congress is difficult to document except as to the experience in the States where such power exists. Those who have carefully observed the operation of Congress know that often a Member of the lower House will vote for a reduced appropriation, thus taking public credit for the economy, while expecting the Senate to restore the reduction to permit the operation to continue. One Senator, a member of the Senate Appropriations Committee, has spoken privately of this situation —he had even received telephone calls from Congressmen asking the restoration of items they had voted to cut.

The possibility that Congress could "load down" an appropriations bill with numerous questionable items and "pass the buck" to the President to veto them is very real. Members of Congress could then assert to their constituents that they had voted for what their constituents wanted, but that the President had vetoed it. Griffith, citing the fact that Congress rarely overrides Presidential vetoes, has said "one reason is that certain Members vote for a particular measure for political reasons, knowing that it will be vetoed.

Without the veto, and with a Congress wholly responsible, the result occassionally would have been different."[18]

The shifting of responsibility on appropriations measures has appeared in some of the States where the governor can veto items. For example, in New York and in Pennsylvania, the legislature has tended to appropriate money beyond the revenues of the State and upon adjourning, left to the governor the task of deciding what items are to be discarded.[19]

Increasing the influence of the Executive. Extending to the President the power of the item veto would *ipso facto* increase his powers over that of Congress. An increasing amount of power has already been extended to the President by means of various enabling acts, yet Congress has managed to keep its basic power by holding its rights over spending. President Taft was especially cautious about the item veto. In 1915, he wrote that

> While for some purpose, it would be useful for the Executive to have the power of partial veto, if we could always be sure of its wise and conscientious exercise, I am not entirely sure that it would be a safe provision. It would greatly enlarge the influence of the President, already large enough from patronage and party loyalty and other causes.[20]

President Taft recognized the reasoning in favor of an item veto:

> The lack of such a power in the President has enabled Congress, at times, to bring to bear a pressure on him to permit legislation to go through that otherwise he would veto. Appropriation bills are necessary for the life of the government, and if Congress, by putting a 'rider' of general legislation on one of these, says, 'We will throttle the government, unless you consent to this,' it puts the President in an awkward situation. . . . Still, I think the power to veto items in an appropriation bill might give too much power to the President over Congressmen.[21]

The item veto would give the President a tremendous bargaining lever with Members of Congress. The President could intimate to a Member of Congress: "If you do not vote in favor of administration proposals, I will eliminate the appropriation for construction of new battleships in the Navy yard located in your district, or for the slum-clearance project for your constituents, or for the new post office building. The President already has many means to help him dominate Members of Congress—through patronage, party leadership, and direct appeal to all the people. To give to the President the additional power of vetoing items and sections of appropriation bills would enable a President to control Congress much more effectively than is now possible.

That the item veto would destroy the system of checks and balances has been argued by Edward C. Mason, who has said that it—

> ... would practically destroy the only power which Congress now has over the President, apart from impeachment. The only coercion which Congress can make use of against the President, except by impeachment, is by tacking measures distasteful to the President to general appropriation bills, hoping in this way to compel him to assent to measures which, if presented on their own merits, would surely be vetoed. This power of coercion would be removed by the contemplated amendment.[22]

Mason overlooked the congressional power to investigate, yet certainly a Presidential item veto would strengthen the President at the expense of Congress.

Mason has also argued that the item veto would violate the principle of the separation of powers, since the veto itself is an exercise of the legislative power.[23] Let us consider this. To allow the President to say that one city can have a post office, that another city cannot, that still a third city can, in the absence of congressional authorization, is to confer on the President an extremely broad type of legislative discretion. He could exercise this veto almost with impunity, when his own party is in control of Congress. It would be very difficult to round up two-thirds of the Members of both Houses to vote to override the veto of a small item for some post office in a community which to them is merely a point on the map in some State hundreds of miles away. Only on rare occasions has Congress chosen to override the President—even when he has vetoed an entire bill of general interest to the country at large. To expect two-thirds of the Members of each House of Congress to take up their cudgels and fight for an appropriation of interest to only one small locality is unrealistic.

Thus, we begin to perceive something of the nature of legislation —the coalescence of policies and programs emanating from 50 States and 435 congressional districts. Such a coalescence of policies is infinitely more rar-reaching than merely local or regional projects. Amounts provided for various agricultural programs, slum clearance, national defense, and a host of other items are placed in a democratic and regional balance by Congress. To permit an upsetting of this is to upset the balance of an entire appropriations bill. This is what is meant by the argument that an item veto could defeat the legislative intent of Congress. One of the most succinct expressions of the nature of appropriations as it relates to the proposal for an item veto is a statement in a House report many years ago:

> Where Congress has appropriated for A and for B, Congress means to say that it gives to each, conditioned upon the gift to the other, and that it gives to neither unless it gives to both. That is the just interpretation of its act, and in most cases is the just discharge of its duty to each and all. The new veto power proposed would give the President the right by the veto of one and the approval of the other, when Congress has only given it conditioned upon the appropriation to the other. The will of Congress has never been expressed on the President's proposal to give an independent appropriation to any one object. The President takes the initiative—proposes an independent appropriation; and the independent appropriation, upon which Congress has expressed no purpose, becomes law by the President's will, unless overruled by two-thirds of each House of the legislative department. The President originates an appropriation, not suggested by Congress, and makes it law, if more than one-third of either House agrees with him. That one-third may be in the Senate, and may be composed of States which number but 5,000,000 people, or one-twelfth of the population of the Union. And so by the will of one-twelfth of the people in only one House of Congress, concurring with the will of the President, money will be appropriated from the Treasury, against (it may be) the unanimous wish of the House of Representatives, and nearly two-thirds of the Senate.[24]

The lack of need. Arguments that the item veto is unnecessary are based on (1) the passage of the "Lame Duck" amendment, which would permit the President to veto an appropriation bill and still permit time for its reconsideration before the close of a session of Congress; (2) the fact that the President can make known his objections and exert influence to prevent objectionable features before they are passed; and (3) the fact that appropriations are permissive rather than mandatory.

Even before passage of the "Lame Duck" amendment, a President could, of course, veto an entire appropriations bill on the grounds that it contained items which were objectionable to him. This was not then, and still is not, an easy course where delayed actions impeded the normal operations of government—a point upon which rests the major argument for the item veto. Nevertheless, Presidents Hayes and Wilson vetoed major appropriations bills because of objections to specific items. President Eisenhower vetoed one in 1958. In other cases, the threat of the general veto has served the purpose.[25] The threat of a veto is one of the means by which the President can make known his objections and exert influence to prevent objectionable features before they are passed. The general range of the President's use of influence stretches across the entire list of the presidential powers, formal and informal.

The third point mentioned above, that appropriations are permissive rather than mandatory, is not always understood. It should be discussed in connection with another point; namely, that items, especially in so-called pork barrel appropriations, rarely represent items at all, but, rather, are lump-sum amounts. The item, rivers and harbors and flood control, in the Civil Functions of the Army appropriation bill, may amount to as much as $500,000,000. The individual project allocation is set forth in committee reports, which indicate legislative intent but do not have the force of law. This raises, first of all, the question about just how useful a tool the item veto would be for the President. Charles S. Hyneman has pointed out that

> Even if the President had authority to make his veto applicable to particular items in appropriation measures, it is questionable whether he would be able to make effective use of it. Many State legislatures itemize appropriations in considerable detail. The governor who has the item veto is thus enabled to disapprove specific amounts for specific purposes, with no adverse effect on the amounts provided for other purposes. Congress, on the other hand, rarely breaks the appropriation down into small enough items to enable the President to pick out and kill what he does not like without also killing many other things that he wants to keep alive.[26]

Moreover, appropriations give authority to spend; they do not direct that expenditures be made. As Griffith has pointed out, "Occasionally the President diverts, or leaves unused funds appropriated for some specific purpose of which he does not approve."[27] Thus the President has a tremendous amount of discretion in expenditures and can obtain the effect of the item veto by administrative policies. Three instances, although there are many, have dramatized the discretionary power over expenditures in recent years: (1) When an appropriations bill rider providing for a loan to Spain was passed in 1950, President Truman disposed of it simply by announcing that he would not proceed with the loan. (2) In 1949, Congress voted funds for a 70-group Air Force. The President was opposed to that policy, and he "item vetoed" the appropriation by impounding the funds authorized and refusing to spend them. (3) When the Korean war broke out, the President issued an Executive order freezing appropriations on construction projects except those essential to the defense effort.

The federal budget system makes direct provision for the Presidential impounding of agency funds.[28] The Bureau of the Budget has justified this power (in acting on behalf of the President) to place appropriated money in reserve as follows:

> In requiring that moneys be placed in reserve, the Bureau proceeds also on the principle that ordinarily an appropriation is merely an authorization and not a mandate to spend money for the specified purpose. This principle has been recognized and affirmed by the Court of Claims in Hukill v. United States (26 Ct. Cl. 316). In the former case the Court said:
> "An appropriation by the Congress of a given sum of money for a named purpose is ... simply legal authority to apply so much of any money in the Treasury to the indicated object."

President Franklin Roosevelt, in asserting this power, did not claim its extensiveness to be equal to the power of an item veto. But, in a letter to Senator Richard Russell, of Georgia, dated August 18, 1942, he asserted: "the mere fact that Congress, by the appropriation process, has made available specified sums for the various programs and functions of the Government is not a mandate that such funds must be fully expended."

In his 1942 Budget Message, President Roosevelt said: "During this period of national emergency it seems appropriate to defer construction projects that interfere with the defense program by diverting manpower and materials." Again in the 1943 message the President stated:

> The public works program is being fully adjusted to the war effort. The general program of 578 million dollars includes these projects necessary for increasing production of hydroelectric power, for flood control, and for river and harbor work related to military needs. Federal aid for highways will be expended only for construction essential for strategic purposes. ... For all other Federal construction I am restricting expenditures to those active projects which cannot be discontinued without endangering the structural work now in progress.

Thereafter, in a letter to the Secretary of War, dated April 28, 1942, the President requested that the Department, "in cooperation with the Director of the Bureau of the Budget, establish reserves in the amount that can be set aside at this time by the deferment of construction projects not essential to the war effort. . . ."[29]

Amounts which were held in reserve by the President have not been insignificant. In the years 1940 to 1943, such sums ranged from $174,000,000 to $405,000,000.[30]

These policies of holding funds in reserve were not popular in Congress, and in late 1943 the Senate wrote into the First Supplemental National Defense Appropriation Act, 1944, a proviso attempting to curb the President's powers to hold appropriated moneys in reserve. This proviso read:

> That no appropriation or part of any appropriation heretofore, herein, or hereafter made available for any executive department or independent establishment to construct any particular project shall be impounded, or held as a reserve, or used for any other purpose, except by direction of the Congress, and any part of such appropriation not needed to complete such projects, or the part thereof for which appropriation has been made, shall be retained by the Treasury.[31]

The proviso was deleted by the Conference Committee after the Director of the Budget Bureau sent a letter to the chairman of both appropriations committees justifying the need for the Presidential reserve power on the basis of sound executive management and savings in expenditures.

An uncertain grant of power. The language of the usual amendments designed to confer on the President the power to veto items or provisions in appropriation bills has been given varying interpretations in the several States. Seemingly an authorization "to disapprove of any item of any bill making appropriations of money, embracing distinct items" would require little judicial construction. Yet such phrases have given rise to litigation in several States.[32] For example, the Pennsylvania Supreme Court has construed the expression "to disapprove of any item" to include the right "to reduce any item." In that case[33] the Pennsylvania governor merely reduced the entire appropriation by one-eleventh. The Court held that such proceedings were proper under an authorization "to disapprove of any item." The Supreme Court of the United States might place a similar interpretation on such language. In this case, the President could modify legislative appropriations almost at will, deleting some items, reducing others, and approving the remainder. This would in effect shift control of the purse strings of the government from Congress to the Executive.

Perhaps the word "item" itself would result in no ambiguity. However, the State courts have disagreed radically in their interpretation of what constitutes an "item" in an appropriation bill. A few of the problems which can arise in this connection will be apparent if one analyzes a hypothetical appropriations bill. Suppose in an Interior Department Appropriation act, Congress, authorized, "in all," "not to exceed" $2,606,475 for 19 nonreservation Indian boarding schools as follows: "Phoenix, Arizona: for four hundred and seventy five pupils, including not to exceed $1,500 for printing and issuing school paper, $168,625; for pay of superintendent, drayage and general repairs and improvements, $25,000; in all $193,625; "Sherman Institute, Riverside, California: for six hundred and fifty pupils," etc.

Suppose these sums were part of the appropriation made for the Bureau of Indian Affairs, a unit of the Department of the Interior. Under an amendment authorizing the President to approve or disapprove of "items" in an appropriations bill, could the President veto the appropriation of $1,500 for printing at Phoenix; or would he have to veto the entire sum of $193,625 allocated to the Phoenix school; or would it be necessary to veto the entire "in all" appropriations of $2,606,475 for the nonreservation boarding schools? Had Congress provided an "in all" appropriation of $30,000,000 for the Bureau of Indian Affairs and then proceeded to enumerate the schools, would it be necessary to veto the entire appropriation of the Bureau in order to disapprove of the $1,500 for printing at Phoenix? In other words, what appropriations in this bill are "items"—the minute sums included under such clauses as "provided that not to exceed" or the "in all" appropriation for particular units? The State courts, when confronted with this problem, have arrived at irreconcilable conclusions. For example, the Oklahoma court[34] held that a bill making an appropriation for the State university, and apportioning various sums out of the appropriation for specific purposes in connection with the operation of the university, embraced only a single item, and that a constitutional provision permitting the governor to disapprove any item in an appropriation bill embracing distinct items did not apply to a bill containing only a single item, with directions as to how that item should be expended, so did not apply to the governor's attempt to cut down a few of the sums apportioned out of the single item of appropriation.

In an Illinois case[35] where an act making an appropriation for the State Board of Agriculture, the State Beekeepers' Association, and other named associations, appropriated to the Board of Agriculture a gross sum, "to be used as follows," enumerating forty-four separate purposes, opposite each of which a specified amount was set down—it was held that the gross amount was not to be regarded as a single item, embracing what followed as directions as to how it should be used; but that each of the "purposes" constituted an "item."

If the Supreme Court of the United States were to follow the Oklahoma decision, it would be necessary for the President to veto the "in all" item of $2,606,475 appropriation for nineteen schools should he desire to eliminate the $1,500 printing item for Phoenix. On the other hand, were the Supreme Court to follow the Illinois conception of what constitutes an "item," it would be impossible to enact dependent or conditional appropriations. Such an interpretation would, furthermore, furnish the President with almost unlimited power. Every single individual item of interest to a Congressman's district or State could be deleted, requiring a two-thirds vote to get it re-approved. He could exercise the power purely for partisan purposes and/or to whip any and all Congressmen into line for his program.

Summary.[36] Proposals to extend the veto power of the President by permitting him to veto individual items in appropriations bills have periodically come before Congress and the country for nearly a century. Perhaps the main reason for their failure to be adopted lies with the reluctance of Congress to reduce its own powers vis-à-vis the President, but there are also many substantive reasons why such proposals should not be accepted.

By his authority to impound appropriations, the President already has greater power over specific spending programs than even an item veto could give him. Congress can override a veto, but cannot force a President to spend all sums appropriated except by coercion—refusal to act on Presidential requests, excessive investigations, and the like. Of course, Congress could carry out impeachment proceedings against the President, but this would involve his total record, which would confuse a specific issue of a particular expenditure which Congress sought to force. Thus, giving the President an item to veto would not provide him with additional authority. Rather, it would give him greater political justification for using the authority he already possesses. This additional justification is the equivalent of additional power, however, and would result in a lessening of congressional prerogatives works successfully.

Proponents of the item veto point out that it works successfully in 39 States. The point is valid only if we are willing for Congress to have its influence reduced to the status of a State legislature and give up its primary responsibility for spending policies. In this case, Congress could then load down appropriations bills with pet projects, passing the buck to the President to weed them out, and leaving the responsibility for appropriations almost entirely with the President.

The item veto could give almost total spending power to the President, depending on what is meant by an item. If by vetoing an item, we mean that he must eliminate actual parts of a bill, then he would be forced to eliminate entire programs by its use. For example, appropriations for rivers and harbors projects are often included in an appropriations bill as a single item. To veto it would mean stopping the entire program rather than merely cutting out a specific project.

If, on the other hand, the item veto means the power to alter items, as it does in some States, then congressional spending power is passed over almost completely to the President. He could reduce items at will, cutting those he did not favor, and leaving those which were a part of his administrative policies. And he could do so with the justification of his power of the item veto.

Since money is the lifeblood of policies, the item veto would give almost complete power to the President at the expense of Congress. This would vitiate our system of separation of powers and checks and balances. It is doubtful that we are ready and willing to take such a step.

According to a previously cited House report,

> These objections to the proposition are fatal to it. They are apparent on the surface of the question; but he knows but little of human affairs and has but little experience of the unseen and invisible consequences of political empiricism who does not shrink from trying

this experiment, which, once adopted cannot be recalled; and the operation of which in the machinery of the Government is concealed from our knowledge; especially when the proposition disturbs the balance between executive and legislative power over money, and vests in the former a controlling authority over the action of the letter, unknown in our constitutional history and dangerous to the equality of right and privilege, or burden and benefit of the members of our Union.[87]

The item veto, then, is a subject primarily for academic discussion. If it gives the President more power, Congress will fight it—hardly providing an opportunity for a two-thirds majority necessary to put it before the States. If the President already possesses the power by means of impounding funds, then he has no need for it anyway. Perhaps these two points contradict each other. If so, it makes little difference since both points work against the adoption of the item veto to such an extent that it cannot be adoped in the foreseeable future.

Chapter **11**

Help Instead of Hunches

The two main proposals for providing better facilities to help Members of Congress pass on spending requests are to create a Joint Committee on the Budget and to permit the General Accounting Office to make expenditures analyses on a continuing basis.

Joint Committee on the Budget

Professor Avery Leiserson credits the origination of the idea for a Joint Committee on the Budget to the Connecticut Public Expenditures Council and the United States Chamber of Commerce. Proposals along these lines first achieved substance in Section 138 of the Legislative Reorganization Act of 1946. It provided for a Joint Committee on Fiscal Policy, consisting of the two Revenue and Appropriations Committees of each House to meet and report to their respective Houses not later than February 15 in each regular session a budget report and concurrent resolution based on the reports. Both the report and the resolution were to contain a determination of anticipated appropriation and revenue totals for the ensuing fiscal year. Section 138 further provided:

> If the estimated receipts exceed the estimated expenditures such report shall contain a recommendation for a reduction in the public debt.... The report shall be accompanied by a concurrent resolution adopting such budget and fixing the maximum amount to be appropriated for expenditure in such year. If the estimated expenditures exceed the estimated receipts, the concurrent resolution shall include a section substantially as follows: "That it is the sense of the Congress that the public debt shall be increased in an amount equal to the amount by which the estimated expenditures for the ensuing fiscal year exceed the estimated receipts, such amount being $...."

The purpose of Section 138 was to fill the gap created by the absence of congressional procedure for arriving at a single, integrated fiscal program. According to Leiserson, the new device was based upon three ideas:

1. The Joint Committee should arrive at the proper over-all relationships between appropriations and revenues on the basis of a month's deliberations before the Appropriations Subcommittees have completed their hearings and review of the President's estimates.
2. The Joint Committee's decisions can be made controlling upon the separate bills reported by the respective Appropriations Committees to the two Houses.
3. A statutory requirement of an annual debate upon the issue of reducing or raising the public debt will provide the means, hitherto lacking, to compel Congress to make its fiscal decisions in a systematic, responsible, and consistent manner.

The failure of the Joint Congressional Committee on Fiscal Policy, with its 102 members, is well known and has already been adequately discussed.[1] It grew out of criticisms that the congressional appropriations process lacked "integration" in that revenue and appropriation measures are originally considered by different committees. Despite the failure of the legislative budget, such criticisms are still rife.[2] These criticisms are at variance with the concept of executive responsibility for the budget and the difficulty of assigning to Congress the responsibility for initiating over-all fiscal policy, and the fact that the committee workloads are too great for one committee to handle both revenue and appropriation measures. Let us consider these points.

Certainly Congress by its taxing and spending power maintains power over fiscal policy. Yet it is not equipped, and it is doubtful if it could be equipped, to initiate such policy. It was the discrediting of this very process which led to the Budget and Accounting Act of 1921, with its consequent executive formulation of the budget. In the final analysis, one must point to the single Executive, with pinpointed responsibility, as the preparer of the budget and thus the proposer of fiscal policy. Congress, as the representative of the multitude of separate constituencies, must, in its collective judgment, pass on the budget both as a whole and as individual parts. It must be the reviewer of fiscal policies. This is a proper role, since the purpose of Congress is to harmonize the interests of hundreds of different constituencies, rather than to propose over-all fiscal policy.

Assertions of a need for committee integration in the appropriations and tax-writing processes do not take into account the lessons learned from the historical development of appropriations. Originally, one committee in each House did have jurisdiction over both revenue and supply measures. This system was changed for two reasons: the workload for individual committee members was too great, and the power exercised by the members of such committees was unduly large. The House Committee on Ways and Means, established in 1802, had been fully responsible for both revenue and supply measures until 1865. Its handling of this type of legislation made it an extremely powerful body, according to Vincent J. Browne:

> The members of this powerful committee had beaten off all attempts to diminish their authority until 1865 when it was generally agreed by all that the load was too heavy. As a consequence, in March, 1865, the House created its Committee on Appropriations.[3]

In the Senate, committee arrangements had paralleled those of the House, with the Finance Committee being concerned with both revenue and appropriations. In 1867, the Senate created its Appropriations Committee "to divide the onerous labors of the Finance Committee."[4] Any informed observer, noting the tremendous workloads of both revenue and appropriation committees during the past fifteen years, would be inclined to agree with the need for the separation, committeewise, of revenue and supply measures.

There is yet another reason for this separation, namely, that revenue and appropriations measures are as different as agriculture and banking legislation. It is true that *total* amounts appropriated should be related to *total* revenue, but the revenue committees have but to look at the executive budget to get the estimates of expenditures, while the Appropriations Committees can see at a glance the total anticipated revenues. Beyond the concern for totals, however, there is little similarity between tax and money measures. The Appropriations Committees must study government programs and the social and economic needs for the expenditure of money. The revenue committees, as such, need have no concern for such matters. Instead, they must study the fairest and the most economically effective methods of taxation and strive to enact tax measures which will bring in the amount of revenue necessary to the national economy.

The idea of having one committee handle both tax and spending measures probably grew out of the notion that those responsible for expenditures would not be exuberant and would squeeze down money requests if they were required to figure out how to raise the revenue to meet them. If so, why should not the committees on Armed Services also handle tax bills, since defense spending is the major cause of large expenditures? One could make a similar argument that the revenue committees handle all legislation which requires the expenditure of money. But, aside from the crushing burden of work for a single committee, this idea assumes a degree of irresponsibility among Appropriations Committee members as well as individual Members of Congress which, if true, will not be improved merely by a change in committee jurisdiction.

Emanating from the concept of the Joint Committee on Fiscal Policy is a proposal of greater justification and merit, the Joint Committee on the Budget. This proposal was first introduced on January 19, 1950 by Senator John L. McClellan, Democrat of Arkansas, then Chairman of the Senate Government Operations Committee, as S. 2898 of the 81st Congress.[5] A similar bill, S. 913 of the 82d Congress, would have created a Joint Committee consisting of fourteen members, seven from each of the Appropriations Committees.[6] Bills providing for a Joint Committee on the Budget would create a highly generalized committee which would be relatively unimportant.[7] The real purpose of the proposals is apparently to create a Joint Committee similar to the Joint Committee on Internal Revenue Taxation, with a staff of twenty-five or thirty experts to help the Appropriations Committees in their evaluation of budgetary requests. Senator McClellan implied this in his explanation of the bill. He declared that the appropriation committees were "simply not staffed and equipped to adequately examine the budget." Pointing out that agency witnesses at appropriations hearings have a "personal and official interest," McClellan asserted that their testimony was "ex parte in character." "No one appears on behalf of the legislative branch ... and in the interest of the public," he continued, and thus the "committees are left largely to their own limited resources." It was, therefore, primarily a measure to provide greater staff assistance to members of the Appropriations Committees.[8]

The bill never passed the House, being subjected to the vigorous and adamant opposition of both the Chairman and the ranking Minority member of the House Appropriations Committee (Representatives Clarence Cannon, Democrat of Missouri, and John Taber, Republican of New York). Their opposition was twofold: power to hire additional staff for the Appropriations Committees was already unlimited, and the measure represented to them an encroachment of the Senate on the House prerogative of initiating appropriations measures.[9]

By the terms of the Legislative Reorganization Act of 1946, the two Appropriation Committees can hire as many staff experts as they desire. Thus, so far as being an additional staff aid for the committees, the proposals add little. If, however, such a staff of experts would help *individual Members of Congress*, then the proposal would have substantial merit. For it is primarily the individual Members who lack information on appropriations matters—a factor which increases the power of the committee vis-à-vis Congress as a whole. Still, two problems would arise. First, committee staffs, hired by the committees themselves, are nearly as much responsible to committee members, and especially committee chairmen, as employees of the Bureau of the Budget are responsible to the Budget Director and the President. This problem has arisen with respect to the Staff of the Joint Committee on Internal Revenue Taxation. Second, a staff of twenty-five or thirty experts would probably fall short of covering the broad area of expenditures. Yet a larger staff might saddle Congress with a sizable bureaucracy which it could not manage. Because of the tremendous workload in Congress, there is already a necessity for great reliance on staff assistants for information upon which to base decisions. In general, Congress is too busy to run the day-to-day operations of a large bureau. That is the reason that the Appropriations Committees have not expanded staff operations any more than they have.

In sum, a Joint Committee on the Budget would not do any great harm, might help, but could not possibly approach a substantial solution to congressional needs on appropriation matters.

EXPENDITURES ANALYSES BY THE GENERAL ACCOUNTING OFFICE

The General Accounting Office is the congressional version of the Executive's Bureau of the Budget. Both agencies were created by the Budget and Accounting Act of 1921 to serve as central offices for advice, service, and control—the Budget Bureau for the President, and the GAO for Congress—although both agencies are expected to be helpful to both branches.

Thus the GAO and the Budget Bureau both serve as centralized agencies for advice, service, and control, engaging in no primary program activities but affecting practically all governmental activities. Here, their similarity ends. They are vastly different in size, function, and responsibility. In terms of personnel, the GAO is nearly twenty times as large as the Budget Bureau. As the central point of formulation and execution of the budget, the Budget Bureau, in Hyneman's words,

> has a charge which brings all sectors of the administrative branch and virtually all activities and undertakings of the administrative branch within its area of concern, and it exerts an influence on the making of decisions at every stage of government-in-action from the making of highest policy to the establishment and pursuit of routine in bottom levels of administration.[10]

The GAO does not have such an extensive range but is larger because of its extremely intensive duties confined to policies and practices relating to financial matters. Moreover, the Budget Bureau, headed by a director, is located in the Executive Offices and is hence directly responsible to the President, whereas the GAO, headed by the Comptroller General, is considered to be responsible to Congress. The Comptroller General is nominated by the President, but for a lengthy term of fifteen years with his removal possible only by congressional concurrent resolution (which cannot be vetoed).

If the GAO's policy range is narrow as contrasted to that of the Budget Bureau, its range over financial transactions is at least as great and, at the same time, vastly more intensive. In general, the authority of the GAO over the expenditure of federal funds is derived from its three types statutory authority: (1) *Accounting systems.* The GAO can prescribe the forms and procedures relating to financial matters which must be followed by the executive agencies. (2) *Expenditure review.* The GAO can examine specific expenditures and order correction if any of the expenditures does not conform with the law as interpreted by the GAO. (3) *Comprehensive audit.* The GAO is required to make general examinations and criticisms of the financial phases of administration.

Perhaps the most succinct description of the general functions of the GAO has been made by Galloway as follows:

> The act authorized the G.A.O. to adjust the claims and settle the accounts of the government; to investigate all matters relating to the receipt, disbursement, and application of public funds; and to make recommendations to the President and Congress looking to greater economy or efficiency in public expenditures. The Comptroller General was directed to make special investigations when ordered by Congress or its fiscal committees; to report departmental expenditures or contracts made in violation of law; to advise Congress as to the adequacy of the departmental examination and inspection of accounts; and to furnish information relating to expenditure and accounting upon request to the Bureau of the Budget. The act also directed all departments and establishments to furnish the Comptroller General information upon his request regarding their powers, duties, activities, organization, financial transactions, and methods of business. From the legislative history and language of the law, it is clear that the Comptroller General was expected to be independent of the executive and responsible to Congress alone. The intention of the authors of the act was that he should be "more than a bookkeeper or accountant; that he should be a real critic."[11]

Obviously, then, if Congress lacks its own Bureau of the Budget as an aid in passing judgment on appropriations, it does have at its disposal an agency which should possess detailed knowledge about agency spending practices. The General Accounting Office has furnished extremely helpful information to Congress in this regard. On his own initiative, the Comptroller General has issued numerous reports on financial situations exposed during the regular course of work in the GAO.[12] These, however, have been sporadic and mostly concerned with transactions of questionable legality or practices correctable by legislation rather than amounts of money appropriated or conditions of appropriation. The experience of the GAO and its broad range of activity relating to expenditures have led to opinions in many quarters that Congress should make greater use of that Congressional agency in the appropriation's process. Thus a 1949 House report stated:

> Considering the services offered by the General Accounting Office altogether, the Congress had at hand an instrumentality not only to enforce effectively its inherent power of the purse but, also, to provide information required for its determination of fiscal policy and formulation of related legislative programs to meet everchanging and expanding needs of the Government. Although ... the Comptroller

General now is called on for assistance with greater frequency than ever before, even more effective use can and should be made by the Congress, and by individual Members, of his reports, recommendations, and services. The General Accounting Office is, after all, the agency of the Congress set up for this purpose and should be so utilized by the Congress to the greatest possible extent.[13]

More specifically, opinions that the GAO ought to be more fully used as an aid to Congress on financial matters have taken the form of a recommendation that the GAO be assigned the duty of making expenditures analyses on a continuing basis to enable Congress to have a source of analytical and interpretive data independent of the executive agencies. This recommendation achieved substance with the enactment of the Legislative Reorganization Act of 1946 (Section 206), but its purpose was not carried out because Congress did not appropriate funds to initiate such an operation.

Origins of Section 206

The idea of Congress using the GAO as an aid on appropriations matters probably grew out of the dispute over its functions. Both Harvey Mansfield and Lucius Wilmerding declared that the GAO should be more of an auditing than an accounting agency.[14] The distinction between accounting and auditing, with respect to the role of the GAO, has been drawn by Galloway. Accounting involves the recording of transactions and the making of financial reports. It is primarily an administrative function and should be performed by the executive. Auditing, on the other hand, is the systematic and scientific examination and verification of accounting records and vouchers performed for the purpose of ascertaining the fidelity and legality of the accounts, presenting the financial condition of the government at a given date, and rendering an expert and impartial opinion on the economy and efficiency of the management. It should be performed by an agency completely independent of the executive, as the General Accounting Office is. The two functions should not be combined, however.[15]

With this distinction drawn and with provision for adequate reporting to Congress, Leonard White has declared that proper accountability to Congress for the execution of the budget could then be enforced. Were the GAO to concentrate on auditing rather than accounting, according to White, it would become "an office of administrative intelligence" for Congress and a more effective aid in exercising its power of the purse.[16]

As a result of the hearings on the Legislative Reorganization Act in March, 1945[17] and the Report of the Joint Committee on the Organization of Congress, [18] Section 206 of that Act was enacted, providing for expenditure analyses by the Comptroller General. By its terms, the Comptroller General is authorized and directed to make an expenditure analysis of each agency in the executive branch, which, in his opinion, will enable Congress to determine whether public funds have been economically and efficiently expended. These reports are to be submitted to the committees on Government Operations, Appropriations, and to the legislative committees having jurisdiction over legislation relating to the operations of the respective agencies.

The final report of the Joint Committee on the Organization of Congress recommended "that the scope of the work of the General Accounting Office be enlarged to include a service audit of the agencies of government." Such a service audit was to include reports on the administrative performance and broad operations of the agency, together with information to "enable Congress to determine whether public funds were being carelessly, extravagantly or loosely administered and spent." According to Dr. Galloway, who was Staff Director of the Joint Committee, this recommendation had its immediate intellectual origin in the testimony of Comptroller General Lindsay C. Warren before the Joint Committee on May 15, 1945, and in the discussion of his first recommendation that ensued between Mr. Warren, Rep. Mike Monroney of Oklahoma, Dr. Galloway, and other members of the Joint Committee.[19] This discussion shows that Mr. Monroney was one of the chief architects of the underlying concept of Section 206.

The Joint Committee's recommendation also emphasized the investigative and reporting functions assigned to the General Accounting Office by Section 312 of the Budget and Accounting Act of 1921. These functions had already been brought forward again by a new provision in the Independent Offices Appropriation Act for 1946, which appropriated $67,980 to the GAO for investigations for, and the detail of assistants to, committees of Congress as authorized in Section 312 (b) of the Budget and Accounting Act.[20]

In making its recommendation for "service audits by the Comptroller General," the Joint Committee also took into account the suggestions it received during its hearings from Senator Styles Bridges, Republican from New Hampshire, who advocated establishment of an Audit Division in the GAO; from Mr. Robert Heller, Chairman of the National Committee for Strengthening Congress, who declared that Congress should "insist on current and useful reports from the Office;" from Mr. Lucius Wilmerding, Jr., who recommended that the General Accounting Office be converted into a General Auditing Office with the sole function of "making an audit of executive transactions after they have been completed;" from Dr. Harvey Mansfield; and from Mr. Joseph L. Borda, Clerk of the Joint Committee on Reduction of Nonessential Federal Expenditures. The testimony of these witnesses reflected a growing feeling at that time that Congress should receive not only the "fidelity audits" of the legality of public expenditures prepared by the GAO, but also "service audits" of the economy and efficiency of the public administration.[21]

The idea of utilizing the General Accounting Office for this purpose also found expression in several measures introduced in Congress in previous sessions. Typical of these bills were three introduced in the First Session of the 78th Congress. The first of these was Illinois Rep. (now Senator) Everett Dirksen's proposal to create a Federal Efficiency Service in the General Accounting Office and to appropriate $2,000,000 for the purpose. The second was Rep. Robert F. Jones's bill to appropriate $20,000,000 to the Comptroller General so that he might equip himself to carry out his express responsibility of making reports and recommendations to Congress. The third proposal, also by Rep. Jones, would have strengthened the Comptroller General's powers and would have made mandatory his surveillance of the overlapping of duties and functions in federal agencies.[22]

California Legislative Tools for Expenditure Analysis

Meanwhile, there was a growing movement among the States, including California, Ohio, Michigan, Texas, Oklahoma, Kansas, Nevada and others, to create special staffs to serve the legislature on fiscal matters. For our purposes, the California experience, surveyed by Professor Joseph P. Harris in 1952, is worth reviewing. California created a Joint Committee on the Budget in 1941, a Committee which should not be confused with current proposals for a congressional Joint Committee on the Budget because of the difference in the character and function of the staffs. The California Joint Committee was assigned the task of "ascertaining the facts" and making recommendations to the legislature "concerning the State budget, the revenues and expenditures of the State, and of the organization and functions of the State, its departments, subdivisions, and agencies, with a view to reducing the cost of State Government and securing greater economy and efficiency."[23]

The staff of the California Committee, however, was to be more of an entity in itself than is normally the case with legislative committees. It is headed by an officer with the title "legislative auditor" assigned to the task of making a detailed analysis of the governor's budget and specific recommendations for changes. Numbering some twenty-six persons, a large staff for a State legislative committee, it publishes a report to the Joint Committee entitled "Analysis of the Budget Bill." In 1952 this report contained 655 pages covering 400 items and recommending reductions in 125 of those items.

Professor Harris has described the resulting appropriations process in California as follows:

> This report is used primarily by the appropriations committees of each house. It is not passed on by the Joint Committee but is a staff report for which the legislative auditor alone is responsible. The usual procedure in the hearings conducted by the appropriations committees is for the legislative auditor or his representative to present his analysis and recommendations of each item as it is taken up, and to follow with the testimony of the department officer in defense of his budget request as approved by the Governor. The departments submit copies of their budget requests and justifications to the legislative auditor as well as to the Governor's budget office, and both offices conduct an examination of them. The legislative auditor and members of his staff attend the budget hearings conducted by the budget office and utilize the information secured there as well as their own investigations as the basis for their analyses and recommendations.

The results of this system are similar to judicial proceedings, with the committees acting as judges between adversaries, and the legislature as a whole representing the court of final appeal. There is thus a tendency to ignore items with which the legislative auditor is in agreement, with the committees concentrating on items over which there are differences. Moreover, there tends to be an expectation that the legislative auditor should make recommendations in order to justify his existence, and there have been instances when he has recommended policies in order to achieve reductions. Harris, however, contends that "despite criticisms by executive officers, the system works, on the whole, quite well in California under present state leadership."

Efforts to Make Use of Section 206

Ten years after its enactment, Congress had not utilized Section 206. A 1949 House report stated: "Up to the present time, no appropriation has been made by Congress to the General Accounting Office to carry out this program,"[24] and the same situation prevailed through 1959. At least by December, 1946, General Warren had decided to take action towards implementing Section 206 by initiating an expenditures analyses program among government corporations.[25] The supervision of the program was to be under Mr. T. Coleman Andrews, head of the corporation audit division of GAO, who had been brought into the government service to set up the corporation audit program required under the Government Corporation Control Act. Marshall Dimock, then a Professor of Political Science at Northwestern University, had been hired as a consultant for the program, as of that date.

According to a statement made in private conversation on December 17, 1946, by Andrews, there was a great scarcity of manpower with experience in management analysis such as was needed for the program. No man of any real ability along these lines would be working for the government, he said, since it was easy to make from $50 to $100 per day as a consultant to private industry. Mr. Andrews estimated it would take years to complete the program simply among the corporations, and stated that it was his intention to proceed along the same lines which had proved so successful in instituting the audit program—hiring very few people of high caliber and relying largely upon the services of private management firms for most of the work. Nothing was to be done at that time toward implementing the new program among the old-line agencies.

In testifying in 1947 before a House Appropriations Subcommittee on a proposed $1,000,000 to initiate the expenditures analysis, Warren expressed his feeling that the GAO had been assigned "a mammoth ... an almost stupendous job." Mr. Warren asked the committee for one million dollars to make "a modest start" at the job and for authority to employ outside management analysts.[26] On June 13, 1947, the House Committee on Appropriations submitted its report on the Independent Offices Appropriation bill for 1948.[27] The report recommended "the denial of ... $1,000,000 for a proposed new item having to do with an analysis of agency expenditures authorized by the recent Legislative Reorganization Act. ... The committee is of the opinion that this latter proposal should be deferred until a more complete and definite program can be evolved." In view of Warren's statement (given below) that the GAO had "made a detailed study of the section," the committee's recommendation for deferral of the program "until a more complete and definite program can be evolved" would suggest that committee members who had attended the joint meeting of March 1, 1947 with Warren were not satisfied with his plans. Possibly committee members felt that his approach was too narrow.

Despite the adverse action of the House Appropriations Committee in 1947, the sum of $800,000 for expenditure-analysis purposes was included in a Senate-passed Independent Offices Appropriation bill in 1949, but it was eliminated in conference. From then until January, 1956 no further attempts were made to get the program underway. Subsequent developments regarding Section 206 were reviewed by the Comptroller General at hearings held on S. 913, a bill to create a Joint Budget Committee, before the Senate Expenditures Committee on May 17, 1951. Mr. Warren testified as follows:

> I neither advocated nor opposed the inclusion of Section 206 in the Legislative Reorganization Act, but as soon as it became law we in the General Accounting Office began to look for ways and means of carrying out the desires of the Congress. We made a detailed study of the section and decided that under the wording the sky was the limit.
>
> That was true then and is true now. In view of this, I felt that before taking any action I should first seek some guidance from the Congress or from the committees that we are required by law to serve, such as the Appropriations Committees and the Committees on Expenditures. I requested an informal meeting with representatives of those two committees, and I met on March 1, 1947, with approximately 25 Members of the House and Senate Committees on Appropriations and the Expenditures Committees of the two Houses. We laid our problem before those gentlemen and I think I am safe in saying that it was the unanimous thought at that time that we should make only a modest beginning.
>
> Based on that meeting, I included in the budget estimates for the operation of the General Accounting Office for the fiscal year 1948,

the sum of $1,000,000 to begin the work required by Section 206 of the Legislative Reorganization Act.[28]

Possibilities of Section 206

There is no doubt that Warren's early plan for initiating a program of expenditures analysis was so narrow as to cause grave questions as to its usefulness. If the principal purpose of the program was to be one of increasing over-all efficiency and economy in the operation of the federal government, several years should not have been lost in experimenting with the government corporations which employ only a fraction of the federal workers and which are probably more efficiently operated than the old-line agencies. Moreover, since these corporations were already subject to the "business-type audits" conducted by Mr. Andrews' division in the GAO, there was really nothing new involved since the Comptroller General was already charged with the responsibility of making constructive suggestions in connection with the audits under the provisions of the Corporation Control Act. Thus it seemed that the program was to be started where it was not necessary and where it would provide the least information.

In addition, the policy of bringing a number of private management firms into the picture to perform most of the work could not have been conducive to uniformity in the application of the program. It certainly could not have made it as easy to spot overlapping of functions and duplication of effort as well as could have been done by only one group working within the government, and thus familiar with all its operations. Personnel from private firms should probably have been used only as consultants on problems relating to the regrouping or reorganization of the agencies, not in the fact-finding process which should have been undertaken first.

Perspective on the GAO operations under Section 206 should be maintained. Representative Jones's bill in the 78th Congress called for $20,000,000 to be provided to the GAO for similar purposes. General Warren stated that, after a detailed study of Section 206, "the sky was the limit," and in 1947, requested $1,000,000 to "make only a modest beginning."[29] The total expenditures of the Bureau of the Budget are only about $3,500,000, so these estimates seem grossly excessive.

Again, some doubts are raised with respect to the preliminary plans for the implementation of Section 206 by the GAO in 1946.

PART III. *Potential Improvements*

Apparently, General Warren, by a "modest" start, meant intensive studies of selected agencies rather than of all agencies, making use of nongovernmental management experts. It would seem wiser to start "thin" and "thicken" the operation with experience. In short, it would be better to start on a broad basis, even though the analyses would not be as thorough as possible in the beginning, and then, as experience is gained and new staff added, to make the studies more intense. In this manner, the new group in the GAO could "feel their way" in doing the best possible job for Congress.

There are some qualifications to the use of the GAO under Section 206. The Comptroller General could not avoid some duplication of work done by the Bureau of the Budget, but he should steer clear of competition with the Bureau. For example, GAO personnel should not formulate an independent budget, or hamstring administrative functions. They should stick with purely analytical and investigatory functions to provide Congress with data. If their information were not to conform with that furnished by the agencies, the latter should have ample opportunities to make their case.

We cannot, of course, develop the details of administrative operations in the GAO in the implementation of Section 206. However, such a group's activities should probably include the following:

1. Sitting as observers during budgetary proceedings on the formulation of the budget, being permitted to ask questions and receive information.
2. Studying justification sheets for agency money requests in detail.
3. Procuring information by subpoena if otherwise denied. This power should be given with adequate safeguards.
4. Taking into account the information provided them, study also the laws being carried out in an effort to compare goals with operations.
5. Becoming familiar enough with the details of programs to discuss them with Members of Congress. Information developed should help Congressmen to assess the areas where more funds than requested could more nearly achieve legislative goals, and also, areas where reductions could be made with the least damage to these goals and the extent to which damage would be done, so that they can decide on the issue of effects versus the desire for economy.
6. Appearing at committee hearings to give testimony. In general this should consist of a brief statement raising issues and questions the committee may want to discuss. The group should not advocate reductions as such; only provide competent information. Questions from members of the committee to develop further in-

formation should follow the brief statement. The group should not act as an adversary of the agencies, but, instead provide supplemental and unbiased data which the agency witnesses may omit.

7. Furnishing memoranda to individual Members of Congress on request and discuss budgetary matters with such Members or their staffs in person. This would relieve the Members of complete dependence for information on the committees and agencies.

8. Making use of outside management consultant firms to recommend efficiency improvements, but only *after* staff development of adequate data. Actually, it would seem more advisable for the Bureau of the Budget to make such studies, which are a function of the Executive. The GAO group should investigate overlapping, duplications, and inefficiencies since it would not have agency prejudices working against it. The implementation of Section 206 should not stand or fall on the basis of inefficiency studies, however, since its primary function should be to provide information. Still, if such information indicated inefficiency, the agencies should be held responsible for it.

In carrying out operations under Section 206 of the Legislative Reorganization Act of 1946, the GAO would be responsible to Congress in the same way it has been since its establishment in 1921. On the surface, it would seem difficult for an agency to be responsible to such a decentralized body as Congress—indeed, some observers felt, during the tenure of Comptroller General McCarl, that this amounted to no responsibility at all. Yet the GAO is similar to executive agencies in that it will do virtually everything possible to keep on friendly relations with Congress. The need for operating funds plus the congressional power to remove the Comptroller General by simple resolution insures this degree of responsibility. But the GAO, unlike executive agencies, is not responsible to the President. When an executive agency curries congressional favor, it is usually modified by its being subject to control by the President. The GAO serves only one master—Congress.

Were Section 206 to be effectuated, operations under that section would be carried out, in general, on the initiative of the Comptroller General. However, as is now the case, congressional committees can direct the GAO to conduct specific studies or investigations. The GAO should probably not be expected to make large-scale studies at the direction of any individual Member of Congress. But if Section 206 were in operation, the individual Member should be able to make requests for information which is available in the GAO. That agency presently makes no distinction between majority and minority Members in complying with requests for information.

A congressional budget office in the GAO could provide accurate data during congressional hearings. It could represent the public interest rather than interests of particular agencies and their friends. While it might influence policy, as it now does with its occasional reports, it should neither determine nor undermine policy. It could, however, provide information necessary for a greater degree of control over the purse by the legislative branch. And every Member of Congress, on an equal basis, should have access to the information developed, with staff of the GAO available to furnish budget details to any Congressman seeking them.

Thus, Congress should probably try out Section 206 of the Legislative Reorganization Act of 1946. On the one hand, continuing studies of the executive agencies in operation by GAO experts should help members of Appropriations Committees by giving balance to the programmatic presentations of the executive agencies. On the other hand, making these studies available to all Members of Congress would lessen the power now exercised by Members of Appropriations Committees. Some Members of Congress may be too busy to give detailed consideration and study to GAO information. Nevertheless, the fact that all Members would not use it should not be employed as a justification for denying it to those who would.

With the careful approach and the effective functions mentioned above, the GAO could become a valuable tool to Congress by the implementation of Section 206 of the Legislative Reorganization Act. Expenditures analyses made by the GAO on the basis of broad financial knowledge of government operations, generally, should enable Congress to take actions on appropriations matters with a greater degree of knowledge about the consequences.

Chapter 12

Progress without Panaceas

Throughout this study, I have consistently pointed to flaws in congressional attempts to control expenditures—that is, attempts to exercise the congressional spending power on the basis of relatively predictable results. Now the time has come to make a total assessment of these attempts: whether, on the whole, Congress performs its tasks well or badly and whether some improvements should be made. The bulk of the literature in this regard indicates serious shortcomings, but such criticisms are not by any means unanimous. Writings in the field vary from the sharp criticisms to apologia. Congress itself does not fail to lament its own difficulties, but operating on the principle of legislative conservatism, it generally fails to make significant self-improvements until after these difficulties have become virtually impossible to deal with. Major reforms have come only in the wake of the war-caused turmoil of transacting legislative business: the creation of the appropriations committees after the Civil War, the Budget and Accounting Act after World War I, and the Legislative Reorganization Act after World War II.

Hyneman thinks of the appropriations process as "a searching inquiry into the preoccupations and performance of individual administrative establishments and the relation of what is going on to the public interest, as Congressmen conceive the public interest" and "who is to say that his judgment is better than that of the representative assembly of the nation." Hyneman, however, admits that "the literature produced by academic students of government . . . is generally in agreement that Congress does poorly what I am convinced it does well."[1]

Galloway's evaluation of Appropriations Subcommittee inquiries was that "the questions tend to be of a random, impromptu character . . . Committeemen are faced by departmental experts, schooled in the art of justifying their requests. Burdened by many other duties, committee members are seldom prepared to make a penetrating analysis of the estimates and tend to appropriate blindly."[2] Hyneman asked for comments with respect to his position compared with that of Galloway from two men who had "long been engaged in the preparation of estimates . . . and in defending them before Congress." One said that "reductions and increases are made with . . . astonishingly little knowledge." The other remarked that Galloway underestimated "the capacity of these subcommittees to get at basic considerations involved in the multitude of matters that came before them."

Very few diagnoses of congressional ability to pass on appropriations matters are completely wrong. On the one hand, Congress does a rather remarkable job considering the vast number of issues and problems confronting them. On the other hand, as we have pointed out, much of their action is based on safety first and arbitrary decisions. One thing is certain, however: the problem of congressional control of expenditures does not lend itself to any pat recommendation as a final solution.

Academic studies, especially in the field of political science, are often criticized on paradoxical grounds. Conclusions are either faulty because they are oversimplified, tending to follow diagrammatic lines which "look good on paper but won't work in practice"; or they are so "over-qualified" as to lose their meaning and usefulness. It is difficult for the careful student with comparatively good knowledge of the background and current operations of government to make recommendations without a multitude of qualifications. Yet society is not static and the search for improvements in the operation of government must continue on the basis of adequate analyses and a recognition of practical difficulties.

The role of Congress in the spending process should be one of determining the limits, scope, and direction of administrative programs, and Congress should make this determination in the light of enough data to be able to ascertain the results of its actions. Members of Congress should avoid interfering with the details of administration, but the prerequisite to the exercise of control over spending is often factual and analytical knowledge about such details. Hence Congress should not be denied data merely because of the fear of such interference.

Appropriations procedures, per se, have not appeared to present any major difficulties, but a review of the process points up some rather glaring problems. The formulation of the budget rests heavily on personnel who work on behalf of the agencies. When the budget is presented to Congress, the agencies and the Bureau of the Budget maintain the fiction that all estimates are equally sound, and the requests are explained during subcommittee hearings in a context of justification. Individual witnesses at the hearing usually represent groups seeking appropriations as high or higher than the budget request. In addition, Congress as a whole places too much reliance on the recommendations of its subcommittees, composed of Members who are subject to the natural limitations of individuals, especially when one of their major concerns is the interests and desires of a specific geographical region.

The facilities available to Members of Congress, the published materials, and the staff aids for help in interpretive and analytical data, are rather impressive. A Member of Congress can get virtually any material he desires, and the experts in the agencies, Legislative Reference Service, Bureau of the Budget, General Accounting Office, personal and committee staffs, and private groups as well will help in the interpretation of data. Two main problems remain. First, the Member needs help to determine what questions to ask; and second, he needs access to objective interpretation of the factual materials presented. The agencies and private groups help in this regard only in a manner calculated to further agency or group interests. The Legislative Reference Service is not equipped to deal with policy decisions, and the General Accounting Office, at present, does not make expenditure analyses. Personal and committee staffs, to be large enough to perform such tasks adequately, would necessarily involve staff in numbers too large to be manageable, since Congress is not equipped to supervise a large bureaucracy.

Inadequate interpretive data implies insufficient knowledge about the consequences of taking action—a lack of control. The absence of such information, however, does not lead Congress to abandon its efforts towards controlling expenditures, and inadequate congressional attempts to control fall into several categories:

1. Appeals to legislative conservatism. This is an appeal to precedent, capitalizing on a tendency to play it safe on appropriations issues, with Congress being reluctant either to increase or to decrease appropriations compared with amounts enacted for previous years. Such an approach protects inefficient and outmoded operations and penalizes new ideas at the same time.
2. Meat-axe cuts. By this term is meant arbitrary or across-the-board reductions made without adequate knowledge of the consequences. They may be made by means of lump-sum or percentage cuts affecting all agencies, or applied to individual items in an attempt to force more economical operations.
3. Efforts to reduce overhead. The technique of the overhead cut is employed in an effort to effect money savings without harm to program operations. The difficulty with this method lies with the uncertainty of the degree to which agency direction is commingled with agency operation.
4. Protection of local interests. Efforts to control expenditures do not always involve reductions. Especially in the case of federal construction projects which benefit specific localities, Members of Congress tend to seek greater expenditures. The problem here is one of harmonizing the local interests with those of the nation.
5. Procedural manipulations. In the absence of an effective ability to control spending, the congressional Appropriations Committee will often seek to paint a picture of savings—creating the appearance but not the substance of economy. The techniques include the device of re-appropriation, postponement of appropriation, and contract authorizations which do not appear in the bookkeeping totals of amounts appropriated.
6. Legislative standards. Probably the best general method of spending control takes place when the authorizing legislation sets standards so that Congress can know the consequences of any amount it may appropriate. This device cannot be employed on most spending programs where the problem is not one of standards, as such, but rather of the impossibility of setting precise standards and the difficulties in ascertaining whether standards are being met. Adequate legislative standards are often possible to formulate in the case of grants to States and subsidies to individuals, but difficult if not impossible to apply to broad-ramification programs such as international operations and defense activities.

The techniques of attempted spending control listed above represent, on the whole, logical methods when one considers the congressional facilities for dealing with expenditures. But playing it safe, meat-axe cuts, attacks on overhead, local politics, and procedural manipulations certainly cannot be said to measure up to our goal of taking action with knowledge of the consequences. Of the six techniques listed, only the establishment of legislative standards meets this goal, and this method has limited application.

Thus it becomes necessary to review proposals for improvements in the appropriations mechanism. In this respect, we have pointed out that the use of the consolidated appropriations bill, rather than a dozen separate appropriations bills, creates more difficulties than it solves. Although its aim is to give Congress the total picture of all appropriations in a single bill, this is not possible because of permanent appropriations and deficiency and supplemental appropriations. Moreover, appropriations are not the same thing as expenditures and many devices may be employed to obscure the total expenditures picture. In practice, the consolidated bill is no faster and produces no more savings than separate bills. On the other hand, the consolidated bill holds up planning for many agencies whose funds can be approved more quickly than under the individual bill system, and all appropriations being presented in one measure at one time presents the individual Member with an impossible burden of work.

Resolution of the issue of the item veto involves preferences as to the comparative power of the President and Congress with respect to control of spending policies. Many technical, procedural, and legal considerations would appear to represent objections to the need for the item veto. When these are coupled with congressional opposition to the relinquishment of its own prerogatives, the item veto becomes a subject for theoretical discussion only and does not merit consideration as a practical improvement in the appropriations process.

In view of congressional shortcomings in controlling expenditures as represented by the inadequacies in the techniques applied as efforts to exert control, Congress obviously needs better facilities for the gathering of interpretive and analytical data on spending matters. It needs objective expenditures analyses to help it form an independent judgment on appropriations matters. The fact that Congress is not equipped to supervise a large bureaucracy directly rules out an enlargement of inside staff facilities to perform such duties. The creation of a Joint Committee on the Budget along the lines of the existing Joint Committee on Internal Revenue Taxation, with a staff of twenty or thirty experts, would perhaps be helpful, but not sufficient for the job involved. At any rate, House Appropriations Committee members seem to be fearful of

PART III. *Potential Improvements*

losing the House prerogative of initiating appropriations measures and oppose the creation of a Joint Committee on the Budget as an encroachment on their prerogatives.

Our conclusion is that, while there are no panaceas for solving the problem of adequate congressional control of federal expenditures, the implementation of Section 206 of the Legislative Reorganization Act of 1946 would represent a step of solid progress. Section 206 provides for expenditures analyses to be made by the General Accounting Office for the use of Members of Congress. The current operations of the GAO, with its broad powers over, and knowledge of, agency financial matters, places that office in a strategic position to make analyses which would be very useful to Members of Congress. Moreover, the GAO is a congressional rather than an executive agency so that the limitations on the use of the Bureau of the Budget would not apply. Section 206 has not been employed because of the failure of Congress to appropriate the necessary funds to get the expenditures analysis program in operation.

Why has not Congress made use of the GAO in its appropriations studies? Here, perhaps, we must rely on speculation. Yet it seems quite obvious that two main factors combine to stop Section 206 from being placed into operation: it is opposed by members of Appropriations Committees and it is opposed by the executive agencies.

Members of congressional Appropriations Committees are wont to lament their disadvantages in dealing with the budget requests of the agencies. Executive budgets are formulated and justified by thousands of different budget officers and their staffs, and then harmonized by some 170 examiners in the Bureau of the Budget. This massive effort must be compared with twenty or thirty staff members of an Appropriations Committee who are fortunate if they can keep up even with the mechanics of the bills, arranging hearings, drafting reports, and compiling comparative figures. Why, then, do the committees not supplement Section 206 with sufficient funds? One plausible explanation is that this would, in effect, diminish their power. Studies of the GAO would almost of necessity be made available to the whole Congress and to the nation as well. This might lead to justifications for reductions to which they are opposed, or justification for expenditures they would want to cut. As it is, Congress and the nation must rely heavily on the judgment of congressional Appropriations Committees, and if there is another source of information, their power is considerably diffused and their judgment not so vital.

Informed persons recognize the proper role of congressional committees; they are necessary, but this need not be confused with exclusive dependence on their judgment. Certainly committees must be employed as sifting and investigating groups which are of enormous help to Congress as a whole. Nevertheless, members of committees are Members of Congress. They have constituencies and interests to represent; they are not unbiased; their decisions are intra-committee compromises, and not necessarily representative of the collective interests of the whole Congress. Power in Congress is power to represent one's constituents more adequately, which, in turn, is additional power to get re-elected. It is greatly sought in Congress. Those who have it are largely on the receiving end of benefits flowing from the seniority system. But special power held by members of Appropriations Committees is not power exercised for the nation as a whole.

Similar factors enter into executive opposition to GAO help to Congress on money matters. The executive power over budgetary details is virtually exclusive, and further information to Congress by the GAO would diffuse this power. Congressional information on the budget, the opposition would contend, can be furnished by the Bureau of the Budget and the agencies. The Bureau of the Budget is a competent agency with a trained staff, but it is responsible to the President, not to Congress. It takes no great amount of insight to determine what would happen to a Bureau employee who pointed out soft spots in the President's budget to Members of Congress. When the Bureau's experts testify before congressional committees, it is in a context of expenditures justification, not an objective critical analysis. The Bureau of the Budget is a vital necessity in the formulation of the budget and in its explanation to Congress, but Congress cannot rely on the Bureau exclusively for objective help in passing on spending propositions.

The Legislative Reference Service of the Library of Congress is, like the GAO, an arm of Congress. But this Service, unlike the GAO, does not deal with agency finances on a day-to-day basis. Moreover, the Legislative Reference Service must be concerned with all legislation rather than being confined to financial matters only. Members of Congress in general and congressional Appropriations Committees in particular need more staff held, but this will not restore control over spending to the legislative branch. Appropriations Committees could vote themselves as large a staff as they want. But large congressional staffs are unwieldy for persons who cannot devote full time to their supervision, and Congress must beware, as it has done, of shackling itself with the massive impediments of a large operation.

Providing a staff in an arm of Congress such as the GAO would permit the existence of a staff under Congress without the need for individual supervision by Members of Congress. Moreover, this would avoid the problem of supervision by committee chairmen who must be concerned with a wide variety of issues, including those affecting their own narrow constituencies and interests. While the primary purpose of the GAO has been to conduct accounting checks and audits of governmental expenditures, congressional committees have already used it to great advantage in carrying out investigations of various programs. These, however, have been sporadic and isolated. What is needed is a full-time operation within the GAO which could make continuing expenditure studies of all agencies. GAO staff could analyze operations in relation to agency expenditures so that Congress could have real information about the true effects of budget reductions, rather than having sand thrown in their eyes by the executive agencies anxious to protect their estimates.

Students of government realize only too well the endlessness of the search for improvements in the operation of Congress, and the debatability of virtually every suggestion proposed. Congressional exercise of the spending power does not appear to be in such a precarious position as to warrant desperate, disaster-stopping measures. Some careful students such as Hyneman are even convinced that Congress "does well" in carrying out its duties in this regard. Congress itself has done little of significance towards making improvements since passage of the Legislative Reorganization Act, and thus seemingly accepts the status quo with few qualms. Nevertheless, the preponderance of academic writing carries with it the thought that the appropriations process needs improvement. Moreover, if Congress as a whole has not adopted any recent measures providing for improvement, the appropriations hearings and floor debate are replete with congressional cries for help. And most of the techniques applied by Congress to control expenditures—playing it safe, meat-axe cuts, attacks on overhead, local politics, and procedural manipulation—can by no stretch of the imagination be considered as the exercise of the spending power with even a relatively high degree of knowledge about the consequences of such exercise of power.

Implementing Section 206 of the Legislative Reorganization Act to permit the General Accounting Office to make expenditures analyses for Congress is certainly no panacea. Yet, such a step would provide Congress with a source of objective analyses and interpretative data which it needs if it is to exercise its independent judgment on appropriations measures. Expenditures analysis by the GAO appears to be a better method of helping Congress to control the purse than any of the other suggestions advanced. Thus implementation of Section 206 would represent definite progress towards the achievement of our goal of Congress' taking action on the basis of ascertainable results. Such a course would amount to progress without panaceas.

NOTES

Chapter 1

1. George B. Galloway, *The Legislative Process in Congress* (New York: Thomas Y. Crowell Co., 1953), pp. 91, 645.
2. For a theoretical treatment of the purpose of budget offices, see Paul Appleby, "The Role of the Budget Division," *Public Administration Review*, XVII (1957), 156–58. An excellent review of the background of the national budget system and the factors which influenced the institutional development of the U.S. Bureau of the Budget since 1921 may be found in Fritz Morstein Marx, "The Bureau of the Budget: Its Evolution and Present Role," *American Political Science Review*, XXXIX (1945), 653–84. George Galloway has made penetrating analyses and offered constructive suggestions for improvments in the appropriations process in several works. See especially his *Congress at the Crossroads* (New York: Crowell, 1946), pp. 245–66; *Legislative Process in Congress* (New York: Crowell, 1953), Chapters 5 and 6; *Reform of the Federal Budget*, Public Affairs Bulletin No. 80 (Washington: Legislative Reference Service, Library of Congress, 1950); and "Next Steps in Congressional Reform," *University of Illinois Bulletin*, L (1952). See also Joseph P. Harris, "Needed Reforms in the Federal Budget System," *Public Administration Review*, XII (1952), 243–50, and Arthur W. McMahon, "Congressional Oversight of Administration: The Power of the Purse," *Political Science Quarterly*, LVIII (1943), 161–90. For the 1949 Hoover Commmission studies, see Commission on Organization of the Executive Branch of the Government, *Task Force Report on Fiscal, Budgeting, and Accounting Activities,* and *Report on Budgeting and Accounting* (Washington: U.S. Government Printing Office, 1949). Elias Huzar has made a thorough study of Congress and the military budget in *The Purse and the Sword: Control of the Army by Congress through Military Appropriations* (Ithaca: Cornell University Press, 1950). An historical study of congressional attempts from 1789 to 1941 to control the use of funds appropriated to the executive agencies has been made by Lucius Wilmerding, Jr. in *The Spending Power: A History of the Efforts of Congress to Control Expenditures* (New Haven: Yale University Press, 1943). For a comprehensive study of the entire budget process, see Arthur Smithies, *The Budgetary Process in the United States* (New York: McGraw-Hill, 1955).
3. Stephen K. Bailey, for example, notes the limitations of narrow constituency interests already in operation during conference committee delibera-

tions. See *Congress Makes a Law* (New York: Columbia University Press, 1950), chap. x.

4. "Control" may not be the best term because of its use in political science literature in so many different yet related contexts. In his *Bureaucracy in a Democracy* (New York: Harper and Bros., 1950), Charles S. Hyneman has discussed variants in the use of the terms "direction and control" (chap. iii). He, himself, employs "direction and control" in the broad sense of embracing "appointment and removal and every other influence to which administrative officials and employees actually respond in any degree." (p. 39). Because he uses the terms in such a broad sense, the questions he lists as being crucial to the direction and control of administrative officials and employees (p. 43) all involve both Congress and the Executive with varying degrees of responsibility. The most pertinent question we are concerned with here involves "setting limits to the scope and intensity of the bureaucracy's effort to carry out different government activities." We shall use "congressional control" of expenditures to mean not only "setting limits to the scope and intensity" of governmental activities, but also doing so with knowledge of the consequences of these limits.

5. Ernest S. Griffith, *The Impasse of Democracy* (New York: Harrison-Hilton Books, 1939), p. 182.

6. James M. Burns, *Congress on Trial* (New York: Harper and Bros., 1949), p. 115.

7. Edward C. Banfield, "Congress and the Budget: A Planner's Criticism," *American Political Science Review*, XLIII (December, 1949), 1217–18. Perhaps "nonrational" would be a better word than "irrational" since the latter implies a nonuse of reason. Cf. Talcott Parsons, *Structure of Social Action* (2nd ed.; Glencoe, Illinois: Free Press, 1949), p. 66.

8. In short, what may be nonrational for the nation may be rational in terms of the interests served by the bureau. See Paul H. Douglas, *Economy in the National Government* (Chicago: University of Chicago Press, 1952), p. 44.

9. Vincent J. Browne, *The Control of the Public Budget* (Washington: Public Affairs Press, 1949), p. 12.

10. *Ibid.*, pp. 31–32.

11. Alexander Hamilton, "The Federalist. No. 58" (From the New York Packet, February 22, 1788), *The Federalist* (Washington: National Home Library Foundation, 1937), p. 380.

12. Henry James Ford, "Budget Making and the Work of Government," *The Annals of the American Academy of Political and Social Science*, LXII (November, 1915), 4–5.

13. Browne, *op. cit.*, pp. 36–37.

14. *Ibid.*, p. 96.

15. Wilmerding, *op. cit.*, pp. 4–5.

16. See Ernest S. Griffith, *Congress: Its Contemporary Role* (New York: New York University Press, 1952), p. 54.

17. W. F. Willoughby, *Principles of Legislative Organization and Administration* (Washington: The Brookings Institution, 1932), pp. 503–04.

18. S. Rep. No. 1011, 79th Congress, 2d Sess., 29–30 (1946).
19. Commission on Organization of the Executive Branch, *Budgeting and Accounting*, pp. 8–11.
20. Wilmerding, *op. cit.*
21. As Edward S. Corwin has pointed out, wars bring expansion of executive powers, and there has been an historical tendency for Congress to strengthen itself at the close of these wars. See Edward S. Corwin, *The President, Office and Powers; History and Analysis of Practice and Opinion* (4th ed., New York: New York University Press, 1957). See also Roland Young, *Congressional Politics in the Second World War* (New York: Columbia University Press, 1956).
22. Galloway, *Legislative Process in Congress*, p. 141. See also, for example, Roland Young, *This Is Congress* (New York: Alfred A. Knopf, 1943), p. 221; Paul H. Appleby, *Big Democracy* (New York: Alfred A. Knopf, 1945), p. 165; and MacMahon, *op. cit.*, p. 163.
23. Harris, *op. cit.*, p. 250.
24. MacMahon, *op. cit.*, p. 161.
25. Banfield, *op. cit.*, pp. 1217–18.
26. Lord Campion, et al., *Parliament: A Survey* (London: Allen and Unwin, 1952 , p. 161.
27. Burns, *op. cit.*, pp. 116–17. See also Luther Gulick, "Politics, Administration, and the New Deal," *The Annals of the American Academy of Political and Social Science*, CLXIX (September, 1933), 61. See also J. M. Gaus and L. O. Walcott, *Public Administration and the United States Department of Agriculture* (Chicago: Public Administration Service, 1940); M. E. Dimock, *Modern Politics and Administration* (New York: American Book Co., 1937); and Dwight Waldo, *The Administrative State* (New York: The Ronald Press, 1948), all cited by Burns.
28. Huzar, *op. cit.*, pp. 398–99.
29. *Ibid.*, pp. 390–91.
30. Griffith, *Congress*, pp. 111, 112.

Chapter 2

1. The effectiveness of the Bureau of the Budget did not come into being immediately but evolved over the years since its creation. See Marx, *op. cit.*, pp. 682–83.
2. Although the adoption of the tentative or target budget acts as a depressant on vested interest demands for the expansion of various programs, its significance lies primarily in its administrative consequences. It has brought to the department heads involved a new perspective on their role in the budget process. In the absence of tentative ceilings, a department head would tend merely to transmit the requests of his various units to the Bureau of the Budget. Now, however, he must bring his total requests in line with the tentative ceiling on the basis of departmental priorities and develop a unified and balanced departmental program. This has saved much time which was formerly wasted at the unit level in preparing detailed justifications for requests which ultimately

would not be considered. The tentative ceiling has been a tremendous aid to the Bureau of the Budget because it incorporates the judgment of the department heads. This does not mean that new or expanded programs are necessarily ruled out. Besides the regular requests, the departments may submit "B list" items beyond the ceiling limitations. But the Bureau has a clearer understanding of relative priorities under the tentative ceiling system.

3. Rowland Egger, *The Division of Estimates of the United States Bureau of the Budget: A Summary and Appraisal* (U.S. Bureau of the Budget, 1949), pp. 22, 24. (Mimeographed)

4. House Subcommittee of the Committee on Appropriations, *Hearings, Independent Offices Appropriation Bill for 1951*, Part 5, 81st Cong., 2d Sess., 1524 (1950). Cited hereafter as House, *Hearings, Independent Offices Appropriations, 1951.*

5. Senate Subcommittee of the Committee on Appropriations, *Hearings, Independent Offices Appropriations for 1952*, 82d Cong., 1st Sess., 116 (1951). Cited hereafter as Senate, *Hearings, Independent Offices Appropriations, 1952.*

6. H. R. Rep. No. 2457, 81st Cong., 2d Sess., 114, 193 (1950).

7. House, *Hearings, Independent Offices Appropriations, 1951*, p. 1532.

8. Egger, *op. cit.*, p. 5.

9. Senate Subcommittee of the Committee on Appropriations, *Hearings, Civil Functions, Department of the Army Appropriation for 1953*, 82d Cong., 2d Sess., 384 (1952). Cited hereafter as Senate, *Hearings, Civil Functions Appropriation, 1953.*

10. Douglas, *op. cit.*, pp. 58–59.

11. House Subcommittee of the Committee on Appropriations, *Hearings, Civil Functions, Department of the Army Appropriation Bill for 1953*. Parts 1 and 2, 82d Cong., 2d Sess. (1952). Cited hereafter as House, *Hearings, Civil Functions Appropriations, 1953.*

12. Senate, *Hearings, Civil Functions Appropriations, 1953.*

13. Griffith, *Congress*, p. 77.

14. Cong. Rec., 82d Cong., 2d Sess., XCVIII (1952), Part 3, 3641. Cited hereafter as Cong. Rec.

Chapter 3

1. House Subcommittee of the Committee on Appropriations, *Hearings, Departments of State, Justice, Commerce, and the Judiciary Appropriations, 1953*, 82d Cong., 2d Sess., I, 20–149 (1952). Cited hereafter as House, *Hearings, State, etc., Appropriations, 1953.*

2. Senate Subcommittee of the Committee on Appropriations, *Hearings, State, Justice, Commerce and the Judiciary Appropriations, 1953*, 82d Cong., 2d Sess. (1952). Cited hereafter as Senate, *Hearings, State, etc., Appropriations, 1953.*

3. Senate subcommittee recommendations for the Department of State were unchanged by the full committee. See S. Rep. No. 1807, 82d Cong., 2d Sess. (1952). The subcommittee print of this report, which contained the subcommittee recommendations, is not available to the public.

4. Huzar, *op. cit.*, p. 384.
5. Cong. Rec., XCVIII, Part 8, A503.
6. House, *Hearings, State, etc., Appropriations, 1953*, pp. 143–61.
7. Griffith, *Congress*, pp. 67–68.
8. *Ibid.*, pp. 69–70.
9. Galloway, *The Legislative Process in Congress*, p. 42.
10. *Ibid.*, p. 407.
11. Douglas, *op. cit.*, p. 68.
12. Cong. Rec., XCVIII, Part 3, 3417–18.
13. *Ibid.*, Part 6, p. 7587.
14. Griffith, *Congress*, pp. 73–75.
15. *Ibid.*, pp. 76–77.
16. Cong. Rec., XCVIII, Part 2, 1750.
17. *Ibid.*, Part 3, p. 3627.

Chapter 4

1. Joseph P. Chamberlain, *Legislative Process: National and State* (New York: D. Appleton-Century, 1936), p. 5.
2. Galloway, *The Legislative Process in Congress*, p. 44.
3. House Subcommittee of the Committee on Appropriations, *Explanatory Notes, Department of Defense Appropriation Bill for 1953*, H. R. 7391 (Committee print), 82d Cong., 2d Sess., 6–7 (1952). Cited hereafter as House, *Explanatory Notes on Defense Appropriation, 1953*.
4. Cong. Rec. XCVIII, Part 3, 3626.
5. *Ibid.*, p. 3323.
6. *Ibid.*, Part 6, pp. 8100–07.
7. *Ibid.*, p. 8105.
8. House, *Hearings, State, etc., Appropriations, 1953,* Part II, p. 25.
9. S. Rep. No. 1807, p. 22.
10. H. R. Rep. No. 1665, 82d Cong., 2d Sess., 8, 10 (1952).
11. Cong. Rec., XCVIII, Part 3, 2524, 3544, 3524, 3543.
12. S. Rep. No. 1807, p. 8.
13. Cong. Rec., XCVIII, Part 3, p. 3505.
14. House, *Hearings, State, etc., Appropriations, 1953*, pp. 143–61.
15. Cong. Rec., XCVIII, Part 3, 3524.
16. *Ibid.*, pp. 3525, 3527, 3529, 3530.
17. House, *Hearings, State, etc., Appropriations, 1953*, pp. 101–02.
18. *Ibid.*, pp. 353–57, 362–65, 367.

Chapter 5

1. Cong. Rec., 81st Cong., 2d Sess., XCVI (1950).
2. Griffith, *Congress*, p. 80.
3. H. R. Doc. No. 182, 82d Cong., 2d Sess. (1951).
4. Huzar, *op. cit.*, pp. 374–75.
5. S. Rep. No. 1861, 82d Cong., 2d Sess., 3 (1952).
6. House, *Explanatory Notes on Defense Appropriation, 1953*, p. 7.
7. Cong. Rec., XCVIII, Part 3, 3629.

8. S. Rep. No. 1861, pp. 7–8.
9. See Cong. Rec., XCVIII, Part 7, 8440.
10. *Ibid.*, Part 3, p. 3898.
11. *Ibid.*
12. *Ibid.*, p. 3900.
13. S. Rep. No. 1861.
14. Cong. Rec., XCVIII, Part 3, 3634–35.
15. *Ibid.*, p. 3628.
16. *Ibid.*, pp. 3719–20.
17. *Ibid.*, p. 3627.
18. *Ibid.*, pp. 3621–22.
19. House, *Explanatory Notes on Defense Appropriation, 1953,* p. 6.
20. S. Rep. No. 1861, p. 11.

Chapter 6

1. H. R. Rep. No. 1517, 82d Cong., 2d Sess., Part 3, 9–10 (1952).
2. Cong. Rec., XCVIII, Part 2, 2524.
3. *Ibid.*, p. 2659.
4. Senate Subcommittee of the Committee on Appropriations, *Hearings, Treasury and Post Office Appropriations, 1953,* 82d Cong., 2d Sess., 530–31 (1952). Cited hereafter as Senate, *Hearings, Treasury and Post Office Appropriations, 1953.*
5. House Subcommittee of the Committee on Appropriations, *Hearings, Treasury and Post Office Appropriations, 1953,* 82d Cong., 2d Sess. (1952). Cited hereafter as House, *Hearings, Treasury and Post Office Appropriations, 1953.*
6. *Ibid.*, pp. 1–2, 4–5.
7. Cong. Rec., XCVIII, Part 2, p. 1750.
8. House, *Hearings, Treasury and Post Office Appropriations, 1953,* pp. 9, 149.
9. H. R. Rep. No. 1450, 82d Cong., 2d Sess., 15 (1952).
10. Cong. Rec., XCVIII, Part 2, 1750.
11. Senate, *Hearings, Treasury and Post Office Appropriations, 1953.*
12. S. Rep. No. 1404, 82d Cong., 2d Sess., 3 (1952).
13. Cong. Rec., XCVIII, Part 4, 4488, 4547.
14. *Ibid.*, pp. 8022, 8125.
15. Senate Subcommittee of the Committee on Appropriations, *Hearings, Independent Offices Appropriations, 1953,* 82d Cong., 2d Sess., 798 (1952). Cited hereafter as Senate, *Hearings, Independent Offices Appropriations, 1953.*
16. House Subcommittee of the Committee on Appropriations, *Hearings, Independent Offices Appropriations, 1953,* 82d Cong., 2d Sess., Part 3, 1422 (1952). Cited hereafter as House, *Hearings, Independent Offices Appropriations, 1953.*
17. House, *Hearings, Independent Offices Appropriations, 1953,* p. 1265.
18. H. R. Rep. No. 1517, p. 20.
19. Senate, *Hearings, Independent Offices Appropriations, 1953,* p. 887.
20. S. Rep. No. 1603, 82d Cong., 2d Sess. (1952).

Chapter 7

1. The problem is even more complicated. River projects are carried out by competing agencies, the Corps of Engineers of the Army, and the Bureau of Reclamation in the Department of the Interior, and, to some extent, the Department of Agriculture and the Federal Power Commission are also concerned. This gives rise to jurisdictional disputes and heated rivalries over water policies. These problems are outside the scope of this book and, moreover, have already been the subject of several excellent studies. Cf. Arthur Maass, *Muddy Waters* (Cambridge: Harvard University Press, 1951); Commission on Organization of Executive Branch of Government (Hoover Commission), *Report of Task Force on Natural Resources* (Washington: U. S. Government Printing Office, 1949); and Charles McKinley, *Uncle Sam in the Pacific Northwest* (Berkeley, California: University of California Press, 1953).
2. Douglas, *op. cit.*, pp. 101–02.
3. *Ibid.*, pp. 113–14.
4. Cong. Rec., XCVI, 81st Cong., 2d Sess. (1950), Part 4, 5198.
5. H. R. Rep. No. 1652, 82d Cong., 2d Sess., 2 (1952).
6. S. Rep. No. 1754, 82d Cong., 2d Sess., 2 (1952).
7. House Subcommittee of the Committee on Appropriations, *Hearings, Interior Department Appropriations, 1953,* Part 3, 82d Cong., 2d Sess., 754–56 (1952). Cited hereafter as House, *Hearings, Interior Appropriations, 1953.*
8. Senate, *Hearings, Interior Appropriations, 1953.*

Chapter 8

1. Senate Committee on Appropriations, Senator Styles Bridges, *The Record on Appropriations,* Statement, August, 1953 (printed for the use of the Committee on Appropriations), 83d Cong., 1st Sess.
2. President Dwight D. Eisenhower, "Report to the Nation," January 4, 1954, *The Chicago Sun-Times,* January 5, 1954, p. 13. See also Clarence Budington Kelland, "What's Wrong with the G.O.P.," *American,* February, 1954, p. 26. (Mr. Kelland was Republican National Committeeman from Arizona); Joseph M. Dodge, "The Budget and Fiscal Problems of Our Government," address before the Economic Club of Detroit, October 12, 1953 (printed by the Ford Motor Co.).
3. Bridges, *Record on Appropriations,* p. 1.
4. *Ibid.*, p. 3.
5. *Ibid.*, p. 2.
6. The following summary will give us an over-all picture of the revised requests for Mutual Security as they compared with the Truman requests and amounts appropriated for 1953.

1953 appropriation	$6,000,000,000
1954 Truman request	7,600,000,000
1954 revised request	5,100,000,000
Reduction below Truman request	2,500,000,000
Reduction below 1953 appropriation	900,000,000

Immediately we see that although the revised request represented a huge reduction of $2,500,000,000 below the Truman request, it was only $900,000,000 below the amounts appropriated for 1953. Even so, it cannot be said that this shows the precise difference between what the new administration requested and what would have been requested had the Truman administration remained in power. For example, in the January budget for the fiscal year 1953, President Truman's requests for appropriations for Mutual Security were $7,000,000,000 (U. S. *Budget for 1953*, p. 69). However, when he actually submitted the requests, he asked for only $6,500,000,000, $500,000,000 less than anticipated in January, 1952. (S. Rep. No. 2076, 82d Cong., 2d Sess., 21 [1952]. This reduction was necessary because Congress reduced the authorization.) Would this have been done had Truman remained in office in 1953? The claims for savings made by the new administration assume not.

Yet, it would appear, even if we were to shave the claimed savings of the new administration by $500,000,000, these would still amount to reductions of $2,000,000,000 below the Truman figures and nearly $1,000,000,000 below the amounts appropriated for 1953. But there is still the difficult problem of figuring the effects of continuing available unspent prior appropriations. These amounted to $810,000,000 in the 1953 appropriation (H. R. Rep. No. 2316, 82d Cong., 2d Sess., 59, n. 3 [1952]), but, as it developed, unobligated balances were $2,200,000,000 for the fiscal year 1954 (H. R. Rep. No. 880, 83d Cong., 1st Sess., 2 [1953]). Of this latter amount, Congress continued available $1,800,000,000 (*Ibid.*, p. 1.)

In brief, then, the revised 1954 requests for Mutual Security were nearly $1,000,000,000 less than amounts appropriated for 1953, but $1,000,000,000 more was continued available in unspent prior appropriations for 1954 than for 1953. Thus, in terms of total amounts available, the revised requests were virtually the same as the total amounts made available for 1953.

7. S. Rep. No. 601, 83d Cong., 1st Sess., 19 (1953).
8. See testimony of General Hoyt S. Vanderberg, Senate Subcommittee of the Committee on Appropriations, *Hearings, Department of Defense Appropriations, 1954*, 83d Cong., 1st Sess., 259 ff. (1953).
9. *Ibid.*, p. 161.
10. See *ibid.*, p. 162.
11. *Ibid.*, p. 307.
12. Bridges, *Record of Appropriations*, p. 1.

Chapter 9

1. This relationship was pointed out in 1952 during the testimony of Arthur Altmeyer (then Commissioner for Social Security) in the course of his questioning by the House Appropriations Subcommittee Chairman, John E. Fogarty:

Mr. Fogarty: Under the Bureau of Public Assistance, there isn't any administrative control. The States put up the money and the Federal Government, under the law, has to match it.

Mr. Altmeyer: That is right.

See House Subcommittee of the Committee on Appropriations, *Hearings, Department of Labor Federal Security Agency Appropriations, 1953*, Part 1, 82d Cong., 2d Sess., 230 (1952).

2. During the Second Session of the 81st Congress, for instance, Senator Paul Douglas of Illinois commented on the appropriation being considered for federal-aid highways with this observation:

... the point is that by the system of advance commitments, the Bureau of Public Roads has virtually taken away from the Congress the power to appropriate money. The Bureau of Public Roads makes commitments for long periods in advance. Then, when on the floor of the Senate we attempt to make reductions in the appropriations, we are told that the commitments have been made and that we cannot change the amounts (Cong. Rec., 81st Cong., 2d Sess., XCVI [1950], Part 8, 11071).

During the House committee hearings on the money requests for the 1953 highway program, Mr. Rooney offered this comment:

Mr. MacDonald (then Commissioner of Public Roads) and the Bureau of Public Roads have a blank check, and they accord us the privilege each year of inserting the amount which they suggest they will be able to spend.... We of the Appropriations Committee are confronted day after day with things Congress did, and for which we have to pay (House, *Hearings, State, etc. Appropriations, 1953*, III, 413).

3. See *Charles River Bridge* v. *Proprietors of Warren Bridge,* 36 U. S. 420 (1837); and *Stone* v. *Mississippi,* 101 U. S. 814 (1879).
4. House Subcommittee of the Committee on Appropriations, *Hearings, Department of Agriculture Appropriations, 1953*, Part 2, 82d Cong., 2d Sess., 1260–61 (1952).
5. H. R. Rep. No. 2810, 81st Cong., 2d Sess. (1950).
6. *Ibid.*, p. 18.

Chapter 10

1. See S. Rep. No. 842, 82d Cong., 1st Sess. (1951).
2. Cong. Rec., 81st Cong., 1st Sess., XCV (1949), Part 5, 6903.
3. George B. Galloway, "Reform of the Federal Budget," *Public Affairs Bulletin, No. 80* (Washington, D.C.: Legislative Reference Service, Library of Congress, 1950), pp. 96–97.
4. Cong. Rec., 81st Cong., 2d Sess., XCV (1950), Part 1, 233.
5. Galloway, "Next Steps in Congressional Reform," pp. 19–20.
6. S. Rep. No. 842, p. 8.
7. *Ibid.*, p. 9.
8. *Ibid.*, pp. 7–15.
9. Vernon L. Wilkinson, "Observations on the Item Veto," Legislative Reference Service, Library of Congress, August 13, 1936. (Mimeographed)
10. *Ibid.*
11. H. R. Doc. No. 1, 86th Cong., 1st Sess. (January 9, 1959).
12. As quoted in Wilkinson, *op. cit.*, p. 6.
13. Edward C. Mason, "The Veto Power," ed., A. B. Hart, *Harvard Histori-*

can *Monographs*, No. 1, Harvard University Publications (Boston: Ginn and Co., 1890), p. 138.

14. Calvin P. Godfrey, *The Veto* (Columbus, Ohio: Spahr and Glenn, 1912), p. 9.

15. As quoted in Wilkinson, *op. cit.*, p. 9.

16. Charles A. Beard, *Readings in American Government and Politics* (New York: Macmillan Co., 1909), p. 444.

17. Wilkinson, *op. cit.*, pp. 13, 14.

18. Griffith, *Congress*, p. 27.

19. Wilkinson, *op. cit.*, p. 20.

20. William H. Taft, *Our Chief Magistrate and His Powers* (New York: Columbia University Press, 1915), p. 27.

21. William H. Taft, *The Presidency: Its Duties, Its Powers, Its Opportunities, and Its Limitations* (New York: Charles Scribner's Sons, 1916), pp. 19–20.

22. Mason, *op. cit.*, pp. 137–38.

23. *Ibid.*, p. 112.

24. H. R. Rep. No. 1879, 49th Cong., 1st Sess., 3 (1886).

25. Bertram M. Gross, *The Legislative Struggle* (New York: McGraw-Hill, 1953), p. 394.

26. Hyneman, *op. cit.*, pp. 237–38.

27. Griffith, *Congress*, p. 28.

28. For a careful treatment of the President's impounding powers, see J. D. Williams, *The Impounding of Funds by the Bureau of the Budget*, Inter-University Case Program Series, No. 28 (Tuscaloosa, Ala.: University of Alabama Press, 1955).

29. U. S. Bureau of the Budget, "Budget Bureau Authority to Set up Reserves Against Appropriations," Memorandum, March 10, 1948, Exhibit A, pp. 3–4. (Mimeographed)

30. Letter from the Director, Harold D. Smith, Bureau of the Budget, to the Chairman of the House and Senate Committees on Appropriations, regarding the setting up of reserves, December 13, 1943.

31. H. R. 3598 (as passed by the Senate), 78th Cong., 1st Sess. (1943).

32. The following discussion of litigation involving the item veto of governors is drawn from Wilkinson.

33. *Com. ex rel. Elkin* v. *Barnett*, 199 Pa. 161 (1901).

34. *State University* v. *Trapp*, 28 Okla. 82 (1911).

35. *People ex rel. State Bd.* v. *Brady*, 277 Ill. 124 (1917).

36. See Robert A. Wallace, "The Case Against the Item Veto," *Hearings before House Subcommittee No. 3 of the Committee on the Judiciary*, 85th Cong., 1st Sess., 98–105 (1957).

37. H. R. Rep. No. 1879, p. 3.

Chapter 11

1. Avery Leiserson, "Co-ordination of Federal Budgetary and Appropriations Procedures under the Legislative Reorganization Act of 1946," *National Tax Journal*, I, No. 2 (June, 1948), 120.

2. See, for example, Galloway, *University of Illinois Bulletin*, L, No. 31, 15–16; and League of Women Voters of the U. S., *Mr. Congressman.... His Moneybags and Watchdogs*, Publication No. 16 (Washington, 1953), p. 4.
3. Browne, *op. cit.*, pp. 50–51. As authorities, Browne cited DeAlva S. Alexander, *History and Procedure of the House of Representatives* (Boston: Houghton Mifflin Co., 1916), p. 234; and *Congressional Globe*, 39th Cong., 1st Sess., 21 (1895).
4. *Ibid.* Here Browne cited *Congressional Globe*, 40th Cong., 1st Sess., 10 (1897).
5. Senate Committee on Expenditures in the Executive Departments, *Hearings on S. 913, to Create A Joint Committee on the Budget*, 82d Cong., 1st Sess., 1 (1951). Cited hereafter as Senate, *Hearings on S. 913*, 1951.
6. Introduced by Senator McClellan on February 19, 1951. This measure passed the Senate by a vote of 55 to 8 on April 8, 1952. Failing to pass the House, it was reintroduced on May 1, 1953, as S. 833 of the 83d Cong., jointly sponsored by 59 Members of the Senate. See Senate Subcommittee on Reorganization of the Committee on Government Operations, *Hearings on S. 833, to Create a Joint Committee on the Budget*, 83d Cong., 1st Sess., 1 (1953).
7. See House Committee on Rules, *Hearings on S. 913, and H. R. 7885, to Create a Joint Committee on the Budget*, 82d Cong., 2d Sess., 9 (1952). Cited hereafter as House, *Hearings on S. 913*, 1952.
8. Senate, *Hearings on S. 913*, 1951, pp. 1–2.
9. House, *Hearings on S. 913*, 1952, pp. 34, 42.
10. Hyneman, *op. cit.*, p. 356.
11. Galloway, *Congress at the Crossroads*, pp. 260–61.
12. Between the adjournment of the 2d Session of the 84th Congress and the 1st Session of the 85th Congress, for example, the General Accounting Office sent to the Congress 179 Audit and Investigative reports and also reports on 665 bills. During the same period GAO representatives testified before Congressional Committees on 31 occasions and "participated in numerous conferences with Members of Congress and Committee staff employees." U. S. General Accounting Office, *Report of the Comptroller General* (Washington: U. S. Government Printing Office, 1958), p. 10.
13. H. R. Rep. No. 1441, 81st Cong., 1st Sess., 29 (1949).
14. See Harvey C. Mansfield, "The General Accounting Office," *Fiscal Management in the National Government*, President's Committee on Administrative Management, Part 2 (Washington: Government Printing Office, 1937), pp. 33–62. See also Wilmerding, *op. cit.*, pp. 250–308.
15. Galloway, *Congress at the Crossroads*, p. 265.
16. Leonard D. White, "Congressional Control of the Public Service," *The American Political Science Review*, XXXIX, No. 1 (February, 1945), 10.
17. Joint Committee on Organization of Congress, *Hearings*, 79th Cong., 1st Sess. (1945). Cited hereafter as Joint Committee, *Hearings*.
18. S. Rep. No. 1011, 79th Cong., 2d Sess. (1946).

19. Memorandum to Senator Paul H. Douglas from George B. Galloway on Section 206 of the Legislative Reorganization Act, March, 1954. See also Joint Committee, *Hearings*, especially pp. 528–30, 538, 541, 543–44.
20. *Ibid.*, p. 7.
21. *Ibid.*, pp. 272, 750, 856, 983–85, 1001–05.
22. H. R. 30, H. R. 3275, and H. R. 3274, 78th Cong., 1st Sess. (1943).
23. Harris, *op. cit.*, pp. 247–50.
24. H. R. Rep. No. 1441, p. 21.
25. The information concerning early GAO plans to implement Section 206 has been drawn from a memorandum to George B. Galloway from John Leibenderfer, "Report on G.A.O's Progress in Setting up the Expenditure Analysis Unit Required by Section 206, Legislative Reorganization Act," December 26, 1946.
26. House Subcommittee of the Committee on Appropriations, *Hearings, Independent Offices Appropriations*, 1948, 80th Cong., 1st Sess., 21–28 (1947).
27. H. R. Rep. No. 589, 80th Cong., 1st Sess. (1947).
28. Senate, *Hearings on S. 913, 1951.*
29. *Ibid.*

Chapter 12

1. Hyneman, *op. cit.*, pp. 124–25.
2. Galloway, *Congress at the Crossroads*, p. 247.

Edited by Bernard Harris
Designed by William A. Bostick
Set in Linotype #21 and Lining Gothic
Printed on Mead White Eggshell Antique
Bound in Bancroft's Kennett
Manufactured in the United States of America

La Bibliothèque
Université d'Ottawa

The Library
Uni